London Buses: Review of 2023

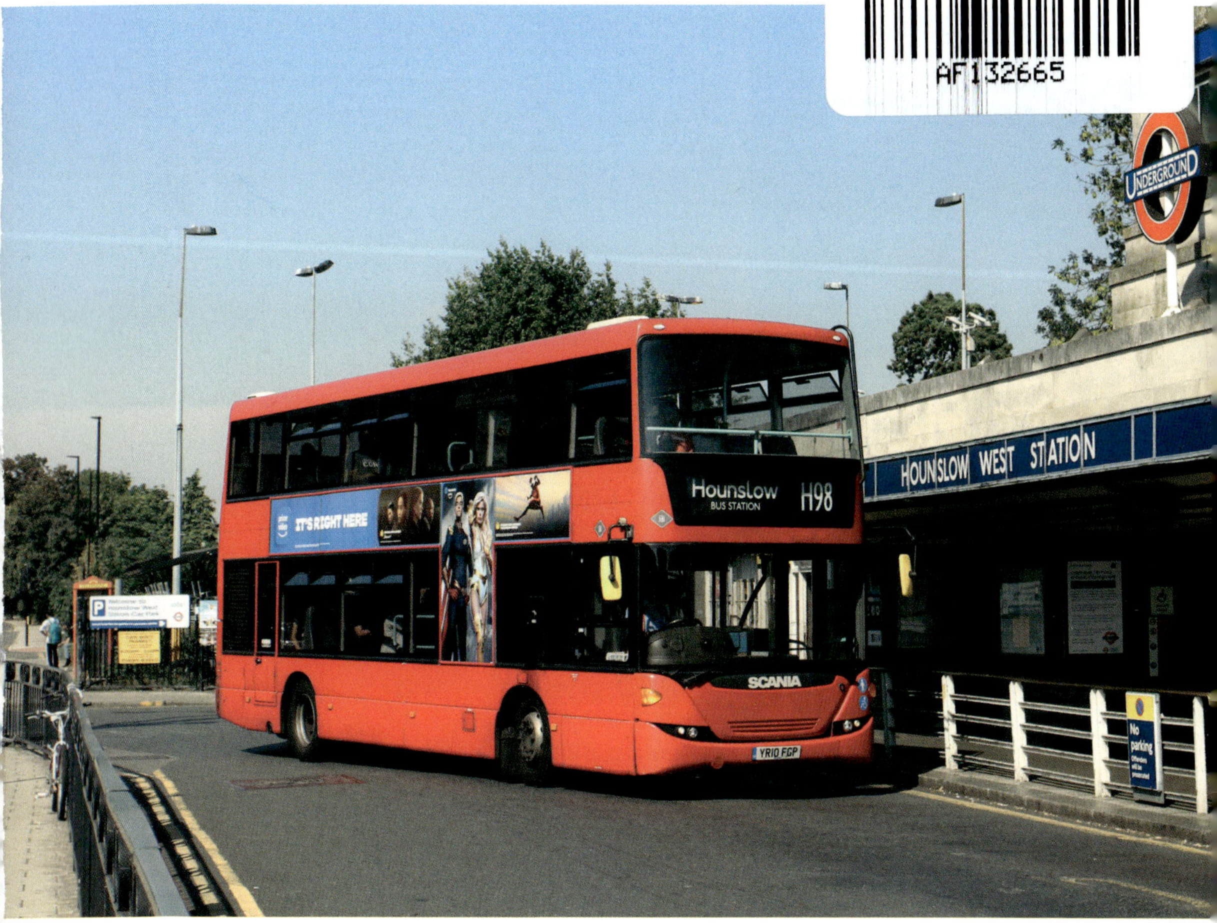

MATTHEW WHARMBY

KEY Books

TRANSPORT SYSTEMS SERIES, VOLUME 12

Front cover: Credit where it's due; Superloop, although a Boris Johnson brainchild, was implemented by his successor as a network (technically, not quite a 'loop' as such) of ten limited-stop express routes. Five of them were introduced in the second half of the year; the SL8, SL6, SL7 and SL9 took over from existing routes 607, X68, X26 and X140 respectively and the SL10 and SL1 were new commissions covering much of the roads of the 183 and 34. 2024 will see the SL2, SL3 and SL5 join them, after which the non-loop SL4 will complete the set. The idea is to have them all electric-operated, but the hurried nature of their introduction has obliged existing buses to step in, with some fleets already at the maximum extent of their lives. The SL9, however, benefited from the newish contingent of BYD D8UR DDs in use on its X140 predecessor out of Sovereign's Harrow garage. Just a top half's worth of vinyl has been necessary to rebrand buses like **BCE 47083** (LE21 FTJ), seen leaving Heathrow on a sunny 5 September.

Back cover: Superloop was undoubtedly good for morale, but London's bus operations continued a precipitate decline in 2023. One particularly unwelcome change that slipped through shattered the tradition of the 11 as London's most natural tourist route. Manifestly unable to keep to time any more in traffic (which continued to swell, regardless of the advent of the ULEZ), the route was severed amidships and rerouted to Waterloo from the west. Bank was thus abandoned after over a century, as in this photo of London General's Stockwell-based Borismaster **LT 479** (LTZ 1479) on 27 April 2023, its second last day serving the area. Accordingly, in the background Threadneedle Street is being pedestrianised, with what buses remained now having to creep round three sides of a square to get to and from Liverpool Street.

Title page: Gradually coming to an end in London is Scania's nearly five-decade contribution, which began in 1973 with six Metro-Scania single-deckers evaluated by London Transport after desperation with the reliability of its Merlins and Swifts. The long-established Swedish manufacturer went on to collaborate again with MCW on the double-deck Metropolitan and, after deregulation tore the guts out of British bus manufacturing, established itself as a competitor for the custom of London's post-privatisation operators, with solid orders thereafter and more than a few devoted fans, who appreciated the heavy-duty chassis' smooth riding. London United under the RATP was a repeat customer for Scania's 94 series and the N230UD that followed it, the latter being assembled at a plant in Słupsk, Poland. The resulting SP class of 2006–10 numbered 206 examples, but all had been withdrawn by the end of August 2023. However, two were reactivated as refurbishment cover for ADL E40Ds, being pressed back into service by Hounslow garage even after their identifying information had been stripped off prior to sale. Thus stark but still proud in this Hounslow West shot on a hot 7 September is **SP 40206** (YT10 XCE), highest-numbered of the class.

Opposite: BYD's dominance of the electric single-decker market continued, with Go-Ahead expanding its fleet past 200 examples in three lengths. With some dissatisfaction with the Chinese products setting in, however, other operators of both the D8UR and its double-deck counterpart have had their heads turned by rivals' new electric models. The 450 was won by Metrobus from Arriva London South in 2023 and set going anew with 17 of the 9.6m D8UR variant, exemplified at Crystal Palace on 17 December by Croydon garage's **SEe 244** (LG73 FYD). Just about visible inside are facets of TfL's new standard interior specification, with high-back seats and faux-wood flooring, though operators are still allowed to specify their own colours.

Key Books
An imprint of Key Publishing Ltd
PO Box 100
Stamford
Lincs PE9 1XQ

www.keypublishing.com

Copyright © Matthew Wharmby, 2025

ISBN 978 1 80282 918 1

All rights reserved. Reproduction in whole or in part in any form whatsoever or by any means is strictly prohibited without the prior permission of the Publisher.

The right of Matthew Wharmby to be identified as the author of this book has been asserted in accordance with the Copyright, Designs and Patents Act 1988 Sections 77 and 78.

Typeset by Matthew Wharmby

Contents

Introduction		4
Chapter 1	Catching Up	5
Chapter 2	Out, Damned Spot!	6
Chapter 3	Chop and Change	8
Chapter 4	Superloopy, Nuts Are We	48
Chapter 5	Advert Buses	54
Chapter 6	Odd Workings	66
Chapter 7	On Their Way Out	72
Chapter 8	Running Days	74
Chapter 9	Tour Buses	86
Chapter 10	On the Fringes	88
Chapter 11	Looking Ahead	94

Introduction

After one of the harder years in living memory, 2023 was generally positive. As passenger numbers continued to rise to something approaching the levels of the pre-COVID era, Transport for London (TfL) generally cut its cloth, though made sure to protest to central government at every opportunity about the perceived lack of subsidy. Savings were made across the board, none of which were particularly palatable; at least some of the large welter of service cuts threatened in 2022 were implemented in the first half of the year, removing from central London both routes and established passenger corridors, while the second half of 2023 was characterised by the imposition of the ULEZ, which was bitterly resisted.

The big event of 2023 was Superloop, explored fully in Chapter 4, but summarised here as the fruition of a long-planned set of express routes. Rider numbers have been more than positive, even if the relentless traffic that the first such routes have had to encounter hasn't done the routes' reliability any favours.

This account hopes to pack in, where feasible, every route change and vehicle addition or subtraction. There is also the usual pantheon of hundreds of allover adverts, plus the myriad of running days enjoyed and finally, it takes a look at what's going on on the edges of London.

Thanks are due once again to the publishers for trusting in this volume and the last, with the hope that all the years up to now can be filled in in the same manner.

Matthew Wharmby
Walton-on-Thames, January 2024

One of the most fulfilling aspects of the modern bus-enthusiast scene is the running day. Each time, there is a new surprise to enjoy from the ranks of preserved buses, reclaimed and lovingly restored to working condition from a time of the owner's choice. This shot of the North Finchley running day of 19 November, timed to commemorate the 30th anniversary of the closure of Finchley garage, shows three widely disparate generations of London buses; 1984 London Regional Transport MCW Metrobus M 1014 (A714 THV), is passing 2003-vintage ex-Arriva London North Volvo B7TL VLW 85 (LF52 UPV), and both are being pursued by something up-to-date, BYD D8UR-DD BCE 47148 (LG71 DXF) of Sovereign's Edgware garage.

Chapter 1
Catching Up

Here are two of the contract changes outstanding from 2022 that didn't make it into the *Review* of that year. One featured, the 248, had its permanent complement in place from the start, while the 307 of a different Arriva London North garage had to start with existing buses and wait for its electrics.

Continuing the drift of Borismasters out of central London after their first decade is LT 138 (LTZ 1138), one of a number of the type transferred within TfL from London United to Arriva London North for the takeover of the 248 from Stagecoach East London on 24 September 2022. It is seen in Romford on 25 March 2023.

On 10 December 2022 Arriva London North regained the 307 after seven years of Metroline operation. New Wrightbus Streetdeck Electroliners were ordered and entered service in the summer of 2023, but existing Wrightbus Gemini 2 DW 515 (LJ13 CCV) is bedding in the route at Enfield Town on 26 January.

Chapter 2

Out, Damned Spot!

Following the spectacular combustion of two electric buses at Metroline's Potters Bar garage on 22 May 2022, it was decided by TfL, in concert with the London Fire Brigade, to add stickers to the front of buses denoting their propulsion, so that the appropriate deterrent could be applied should any more catch fire. Though a little intrusive and adding visual clutter, especially when company logos on bus fronts are starting to fade away themselves, the diamond-shaped stickers, in a choice of four, allow instantaneous visual indentification if fire safety training has not already made itself felt among employees and passers-by.

A simple petrol-pump logo, like that found on car dashboards, surmounts a grey diamond for diesel-powered buses. There is a loophole, however, that ought to have been worked out, in that Alexander Dennis's Smart Hybrid development of the E40D, such as those found on Abellio routes 207, 278 and 285 and Stagecoach routes 25, 54, 75 and 425, are counted as diesels. One of the latter, Catford's 11316 (SK19 ELU), is seen in Lewisham town centre on 17 December.

Out, Damned Spot!

Combining a pump and a flash is the sticker for the battery-hybrid *par excellence*, the Wrightbus NBfL, better known as the Borismaster; Abellio's LT 23 (LTZ 1023) of Battersea garage is seen at Warren Street on 10 June 2023.

Pure electric buses have a flash and nothing else, as on Sutton-based London General BYD D8UR-DD Ee 137 (LG23 FBB) at Kingston on 24 December. TfL's own flash logo already takes centre stage on electric buses.

Hydrogen buses have the appropriate elemental notation on a sky blue background. Metroline's Perivale-based Wrightbus Streetdeck Hydroliner WHD 2721 (LK70 AZP) is at Paddington on 4 June 2023.

Chapter 3

Chop and Change

Chop was the watchword for 2023, but not nearly as much, thankfully, as had been envisaged. Though the central London changes of April severed numerous long-established links, there were bright spots, including Superloop. For aficionados of green energy, electric buses continued to flood into the capital in sizeable numbers, even if it look longer — sometimes much, much longer — to fit out garages with the space-consuming charging infrastructure for them. The next 40 pages show the full year's worth of contract changes, structural reroutings and withdrawals, and the associated replacement of established types with interim existing buses or modern successors.

2023's route changes got under way early with Metroline's win of the 142 on 6 January. In fact, it was coming home to Edgware, which lost it on tender in 1986. London Country and its local successors ran it for an amazing 32 years, but Sovereign could only muster five. With new electrics awaited, ADL E40D TE 1314 (LK12 AWJ) is leaving Edgware on 26 January.

Now belatedly able to take up service on the 125 is Sovereign's BYD D8UR-DD BCE 47138 (LG71 DWV), seen on 26 January having completed the route's recent extension to Colindale.

Chop and Change

The 226 had been won off Metroline West by London United but its intended allocation switched to fellow RATP company Sovereign precisely because Edgware garage was already fitted with chargers for electric buses. Even so, its already delivered BYD D8URs had to deputise elsewhere for a whole year. Here at Golders Green on 26 January is Enviro200 DE 20174 (YX11 FZA).

The DEs already based at Edgware when the 226 was assumed on 6 January 2023 were reinforced by shorter E20Ds no longer needed on the 470 after that route's loss to London General at the close of 2022. On 17 August DDE 20290 (YY67 UUJ) is arriving at Ealing Broadway.

The 142's return to Edgware obliged several reallocations within Metroline. The 32 passed to Cricklewood, in turn ejecting the 316 to Willesden Junction. This route gradually upgraded its age profile through the transfer of MMC-spec E20Ds formerly at Brentford, though a mix of batches prevailed, and even more so when further DELs arrived for the H17 and 223 later in the year. Here at Shepherd's Bush on 29 June is DEL 2261 (LK66 FTA), mercifully not yet subjected to the horrible repaints that went over all the black trim. Later still, the 316 was extended from Cricklewood to Brent Cross West.

A spot of cascades for age and emissions purposes pushed out some of the 321's 59-reg WVLs at London Central's New Cross now that the 264 at associated Metrobus had settled in with its new Ees. The EHs made spare, like EH 237 (YX18 KRK) at Wandsworth on 22 August, thus went onto the 37 at Peckham, displacing several 12-reg E40Ds (Es) to New Cross.

ADL E40D E 246 (YX12 FPA) was of a batch that spent the first half of its career at New Cross, and now returned there to run the 321 in the place of older Volvo B9TL (WVLs). It is seen at Foots Cray on 21 March.

Chop and Change

Most of the planned withdrawals of 2022 were averted, but the plan to remove the 271 after 63 years went through on 4 March. On 26 January, Holloway's VWH 2098 (LK15 CWW), of a holding of mixed batches of Metroline Volvo B5LHs, descends Highgate Hill, which would be covered by a diversion of the 263. Rather mean-spiritedly, the contentious stand at the top of this hill was barred off before the end, denying observers final photos there. Ridiculously, the route's basic form survives, but only by night, through the simultaneous introduction of a night service known as N271!

The 263's removal from the main drag through Highgate was tempered somewhat by extending the 234 to Archway, a terminus it had already served between its introduction in 1989 and 1994. To fill the space at Holloway garage left by the 271's withdrawal, it was reallocated with its ADL E20Ds from Potters Bar, and on 7 April DEM 1342 (LK62 BCY) is coming up to its new (old) terminus.

On 4 March Holloway lost not just the 271, but the 91, which passed on tender to London General. Both changes set in motion a rash of transfers that, in a roundabout manner, freed enough youthful Volvo B5LHs to upgrade the 263 at Potters Bar, whose 09-reg Enviro400s were at the end of their lifespan. Heading north towards East Finchley on 15 July is VWH 2243 (LK66 EDO); this particular addition actually came from Edgware, where it had spent a year after transferring from Harrow Weald.

London Buses: Review of 2023

The southern end of the 271 was replaced by a diversion of the 21 to Holloway rather than Newington Green. From bitter personal experience, this route's extension beyond central London to that point was the only thing that prevented the 141, coming down from the north, from hopeless overcrowding, and indeed the 141 was only half-heartedly reinforced in compensation. On 27 April New Cross's LT 276 (LTZ 1276) of London Central is approaching Monument; this Borismaster had just been refurbished and looks smart for it.

The EHV class's work on Docklands Buses' 135 had ended on 21 May 2022 with that route's loss on tender to Tower Transit, with enough time after that for these ADL Enviro400-bodied Volvo B5LHs to do a spot of moonlighting at London General's Merton, covering for Optare MetroDecker EVs away for urgent attention to the batteries. Now came a new task, the takeover of the 91 from Metroline on 4 February. Northumberland Park could not manage it, so it was put into Stockwell, just as far away at the other end, and on 21 March at Holborn we see EHV 10 (BL15 HBX).

Pedestrianisation of town centres remains a persistent obsession of councils. A side-effect of having removed cars and buses from Bexleyheath Broadway late last century forced routes terminating from the south to go round three sides of a rectangle to stand. This cut into their reliability, so with the transfer of the B13 from Arriva London North to London Central on 21 January a 'remedy' was implemented. New 9.7m BYD D8UR SEe 169 (LB72 DYC) is thus at a new stand at the library south of the town centre, obliging a long walk for older people or those laden with shopping.

On 4 February another reallocation took place at Metroline. Not for the first time, the 107 was reallocated from Edgware to Potters Bar, this movement last having happened on 6 July 1987, but with this particular transfer, eleven VWHs were gathered up from several garages no longer needing them. For our purposes, the route could also now see operation by the MCV-bodied VMH class already based there, and accordingly, VMH 2538 (LF68 PXP) is laying over at Edgware bus station on a foggy 19 November.

Already reduced from half-hourly to an even less appealing 45-minute frequency, the 359 out of Metrobus's Croydon garage now needed only two buses rather than three, and in April 2023 its pair of 65-reg SEs gave way to two newish electric BYD D8URs. SEe 167 (LG22 AXO) is setting off from Purley on 22 August.

The once-large complement of all-Polish Scania N230UDs at London United's Fulwell was whittled down as 2023 progressed, with the last SPs operating on the 71 replaced by Volvo B5LHs (VHs) in April. Prior to that, the surviving members continued to turn out on the 85, as SP 40179 (YT10 XCC) is doing when sighted in Eden Street, Kingston, on 11 February.

The 111 at Abellio's Twickenham garage was due new Wrightbus Streetdeck Electroliners to replace its stand-in Borismasters, but the garage needed to have enough chargers fitted before conversion could commence, so the new buses were initially put into action on the U5 out of Dawley Road, so as to allow that route's existing BYD D8UR-DDs to top up the 68 at Walworth and thus release LTs to stiffen the 111. On 21 March, 3022 (LV72 BZR) is arriving at Hayes & Harlington, its electronic blinds already set for the return journey to Uxbridge.

Coming round the new alignment at Aldwych on 27 April is BYD D8UR-DD 3411 (LC71 KWU) on its temporary deployment to Walworth's 68 while Twickenham was being fitted out for the 111's new Wrightbus Streetdeck Electroliners.

Once the chargers were fitted at Twickenham and the juice was turned on, the 111's electrification proceeded rapidly and all of its new buses were in use where they belonged by the end of April. Serving Wood Street in Kingston on 27 May is Twickenham's 3020 (LV72 BZO).

A lucky capture of two 353s heading for that route's respective termini along the common stretch of road within Addington Village Interchange on 22 August sees new Ees 111 (LD72 YAG) and 108 (LD72 YAA) of the large contingent of BYD D8UR-DDs taken by Go-Ahead this year for use by three of its constituent companies. This batch of nine into Metrobus at Orpington late in March were actually from a different number range than intended, but many of the new buses had been delivered and stored that whichever garage was electrified first got to take them first.

Identical to Go-Ahead's Ees but known by the RATP as the BCE class, the batch intended for the 295 but having waited out the winter on the 65 and 281 out of Fulwell were duly allocated to Westbourne Park during February and March. On 17 December, BCE 47162 (LD72 UFX) is laying over at Clapham Junction.

'Tomatoing', the disparaging enthusiast term for the overzealous mid-career repaints specified by Metroline on its MMC-spec E20Ds, was just as unpleasant on the E40H double-deck equivalent, as an embarrassedly naked-looking TEH 2075 (LK15 CSF) of Cricklewood garage demonstrates at Aldwych on 27 April.

The beginning of the final push against London United's Scania N230UD holdings began on 4 March when the H32 departed for Abellio on tender. Prior to that, Hounslow's SP 40048 (YT09 BND) is sighted between there and Hounslow Heath on 4 February; this bus was withdrawn with the change.

Six months later and a little to the west of the previous photo's location, the weather is much better; in fact, 7 September saw a late heatwave after an indifferent summer, enabling a fine view of Borismaster LT 144 (LTZ 1144), now refurbished and transferred from London United to Abellio to man the H32 out of that company's Southall garage.

The changes envisaged in 2022 were all about saving desperately needed money, and the withdrawal without replacement of the eastern two-thirds of the 427 on 4 March was as extreme as could be, in the hope by TfL that passengers still needing to proceed east of Southall (where it was curtailed from the west) would now be using the Elizabeth line. Coming up to its new stand past Southall station on 21 March is E40H 2563 (YX17 NVE) of Abellio's Southall garage.

Another route to undergo an operator change and simultaneous conversion to what were now mid-life Borismasters was the H91, transferred on tender from London United to Metroline on 4 March. Heavy cuts to the 390 at Holloway had released enough LTs to go through the refurbishment process and redeploy to Brentford; this one, coming up to Hammersmith on 7 April, is LT 104 (LTZ 1104).

London General's closure of Plough Lane garage on 25 March obliged the reallocation of the 485 to Merton. Unfortunately unable to be shown on E20D SE 183 (SN12 AUX) at Wandsworth on 22 August is the simultaneous intermediate rerouting of this service via the new Wandsworth Riverside Quarter west of here.

London Buses: Review of 2023

Only recently ensconced at Merton, the 470 had to leave that garage on 25 March for a new site at Goat Road, south of Mitcham. The application of garage codes had fallen off at London General over the years, but this base was coded GM, in a nod to the long-gone garage at Victoria. Passing through Morden on 25 April is E20D SE 238 (YY15 CNN).

Also reallocated from Merton to Goat Road was the 280, though its allocation became more fluid than hitherto, with its existing batch of 2012-vintage Volvo B5LHs (WHVs) bulked out with whatever Merton, as its operational parent, could continue to spare. On 22 August at Mitcham, WHV 20 (LJ61 NVF) is still carrying Merton's AL code.

The reallocation of the 39 from Plough Lane to Putney garage on 25 April displaced the 424 to Stockwell, though Putney was right on line of route and the new base was some miles away. With only five Wrightbus Streetlite WFs allocated, that was deemed not to be too detrimental, so on 1 July in Putney High Street, WS 81 (SK17 HKA) is sporting a card from one of Stockwell's new spread of running numbers allocated to the route, though not Stockwell's SW code itself; that would come later.

Chop and Change

The start of the conversion of routes 163 and 164 at London General's Merton garage to new SEe-class BYD D8UR electric single-deckers in the last half of April freed its newest E20Ds (SEs) for associated company Blue Triangle to take over the 366 from Stagecoach East London on 29 April. New SEes were also on order for this route, which was run from Henley Road with plans to reallocate it later to River Road when capacity at the latter eased. Here at Barking on 4 June is SE 271 (YX65 ROU).

Also taken over by Blue Triangle on 29 April was Barking-area local route 368, which in its three decades of existence had failed to settle for long with any of the local operators to be found round about. River Road was able to take this on, collecting a handful of spare Volvo B5LHs, though WHV 66 (BF65 WJM), seen at Barking station on 4 June, had been resident since 2020.

Arriva London North's cession of the B13 to London General (see page 12) had freed the seven-strong ENR class of 9.75m MMC E20Ds to at last end the careers of the extremely elderly Enviro200s still operating Tottenham's 318 across the river. Unfortunately, though ENR 3 (LK65 EKR) is well established in this 4 June shot at Seven Sisters, the 318 needed nine buses, so two of the 57-reg ENs had to hold in place!

Outright devastation of central London's bus services, as threatened in 2022, was staved off, but the changes that did take place in three programmes over 2023 were just as hard-hitting. None was more significant than the withdrawal after 57 years of what remained of the Red Arrow network, reduced by now to just routes 507 and 521. In the above photo taken on their penultimate day, 27 April, BYD D8UR SEe 18 (LJ66 CFV) of London General's Waterloo garage is heading into the Aldwych underpass, which could not be served by its replacements and was now wasted. Below on the same day is SEe 28 (LJ66 CGV), laying over at Waterloo station. In early drafts of the plan, the 507 would have replaced the timeless 11 in its entirety.

Taking the place of the 507's leg to Victoria was a rerouting of the 3, which had to abandon its stand off Whitehall; on 27 April Abellio's Walworth-based Borismaster LT 782 (LTZ 1782) can't access it anyway due to roadworks and instead has had to wrench its bulk through an awkward U-turn against traffic.

From 29 April, the 3 simply co-opted the 507's old stand at Victoria, and here on 25 May is LT 776 (LTZ 1776). The Waterloo leg of what used to be a direct inter-station link was awkwardly replaced by diverting the 11 there from the west and rerouting the C10 from the east to go via Waterloo rather than south of it.

The 521 was replaced by diverting the 133 at Bank to follow its former eastern half as far as Holborn, abandoning Liverpool Street. St Paul's, therefore, is a new point for this south London stalwart to serve when ADL E40H City HA 44 (LK66 HBC) of Arriva London South's Brixton garage is seen on 5 November.

Another Brixton-operated route coming up from the south took on the 521's western end, through a diversion at Holborn eastwards via High Holborn to St Bart's. On 5 November, Borismaster LT 979 (LTZ 2179) is on the new section, but it remains glaringly clear that there is *still* no direct link from Waterloo to King's Cross.

The story of the 11 is a sad indictment of how far London's transport has fallen. The brutality meted out to it on 29 April 2023 can trace its necessity back to the partial pedestrianisation of Trafalgar Square in 2002, after which massive tailbacks from the east wrecked any hope of its running to time. OPO conversion in 2003 then wiped out its distinctiveness, though the advent of Borismasters ten years later brought back some dignity. On 27 April Stockwell's LT 65 (LTZ 1065, *above*) of London General is in Fleet Street, which it would never serve again in favour of diversion to Waterloo. The 211, which it was supposed to replace here, has not actually been cleared for its own rerouting to Battersea Power Station, resulting in an embarrassing pile-up of buses along Waterloo's taxi rank. Now terminating at Victoria is the 26, giving up its useful round-the-corner link to Waterloo from the east, and now too long itself. Setting off from Victoria on 25 May is Stagecoach East London's ADL E40H City 12537 (SN66 WSE, *below*), new as CT Plus (HCT Group) 2537.

One critical link unaccountably destroyed on 29 April was that of the 16 up the straight of the Edgware Road, as recently as the 1970s the remit of over 60 buses but now apparently beyond consideration. To sidestep the indignity and resulting bad PR of removing a route number with a century of history behind it, the number was used to rechristen the 332, which did, in fact, restore the 16 to a section of route given up in 1997, but took it off the main drag in favour of a pointless dogleg to Paddington. On 27 April, the rain teems down as Metroline Borismaster LT 543 (LTZ 1543, *above*), with a 332 in tow, is nearing its home garage. After the changes, LT 790 (LTZ 1790, *below*) is setting off from Paddington on its way to Brent Park Tesco on 10 June.

Increasingly often, the planners just don't think. After 29 April there were now two links from Victoria to Willesden and none from Victoria to Cricklewood. The 6 had already been hobbled by taking it out of Oxford Street, but its rerouting via Piccadilly did furnish a new link, and this was retained by virtue of pulling the 23 out of its recent ridiculous contortion back on itself and pushing it onward to its old terminus at Aldwych. However, its removal from assisting the 9 now placed massive pressure on that already heavily reduced service. On 4 June, Metroline Volvo B5LH VWH 2403 (LK67 ENM, *above*) of Willesden and London Transit Optare MetroDecker EV OME 46009 (YJ70 EVL, *below*) of Westbourne Park are at opposite ends of Park Lane.

Metroline's second batch of BYD D8UR-DDs was intended for the 204, but a restriction discovered along that route saw them diverted to the 142 in a straight swap for that route's intended Wrightbus Streetdeck Electroliners, which arrived later in the year. On the bifurcation to and from its home garage at Edgware midway through the 142's path to Brent Cross on 6 July is BDE 2752 (LG22 AXF).

Merton-based London General routes 163 and 164 were converted to new SEe-class BYD D8UR electrics between 17 and 29 April, freeing E20Ds (SEs) for other work. Getting going from Wimbledon on 27 April is SEe 195 (LG23 FKX).

Unaccountably demoted to single-deck since 1996, the 164 was specified to continue in this mode for its retention under London General, and put into service new BYD D8URs like Merton's SEe 194 (LG23 FKW), seen on the southbound bore of Sutton's one-way system on 22 August.

Ever busy and gifted with additional resources by comparison with those bleeding out of central London routes, the 93 of London General began its conversion to BYD D8UR-DD electrics from mid-April onwards, sharing a large influx of Ees into Sutton with routes 80, 154 and 213. Coming round Wimbledon's perfunctory one-way system on 27 April is Ee 113 (LG23 FFV).

Sutton's 154 also traded its decade-established DOE fleet for new Ees during the spring and summer of 2023. Here at West Croydon on 22 August is Ee 123 (LG23 FGJ).

The 151 was also meant for upgrading to Ees to accompany its retained London General contract out of Sutton garage, but a problem was discovered at this route's Worcester Park terminus whereby the long overhang of the new electrics would ground on the way out of the station layby. Thus did the Ees filter onto the 213 (which was expecting its own contingent in due course anyway) and DOEs had to stay put on the 151. Here on the stand in question on Christmas Eve is DOE 49 (LX09 AXZ).

This year, Stagecoach head office decided to separate out the growing number of electric double-deckers into their own numeric batch, mindful that the 14,000s would soon be running out if the existing level of intake were maintained. Thus did every unit owned add 70,000 to its fleetnumber, including the two BYD D8UR-DDs already inherited when Stagecoach East London took over HCT Group at the end of 2022. Thus was the original 2550, familiar on school route 616 and seen here on the regular 20 at Walthamstow Central on 29 December, renumbered from 14173 to 84173 (LG21 HZM).

Stagecoach's electric single-deckers were similarly treated. One of the five BYD D8URs resident on the 323 out of West Ham, 64203 (LF20 XKS) was renumbered from 29203 and is seen coming into Canning Town bus station on 7 September. No further examples of this type have been ordered, Stagecoach East London deciding instead to take a punt on the untried but brand new Volvo BZL model for its contract on the 276.

The nine new electrics to Abellio's recent preference retained their intended numbers, but were licensed after the 1 March registration-number change, so had to void their booked 72-registrations. Croydon's 1543 (BV23 ZZG), entering the town centre of that name on the 433 on 22 August, also demonstrates Toyota's increasing say in the badging of what was previously known as the Caetano e.City Gold. In any case, subsequent electric single-deckers ordered by Abellio have comprised two lengths of Switch MetroCity EVs.

On 10 June Metroline closed King's Cross garage, reallocating the 30 and 274 to Holloway. Showing off the new running-number sequence introduced after the transfer is Volvo B5LH VMH 2459 (LK18 AMV), leaving Euston on the first day, though HT codes will follow later.
The VMHs were a permanent allocation, but a pool with its former parent allowed the latter's VWHs to make appearances.

Now based at Holloway with the 274 (and 30) ex-King's Cross, Volvo B5LH VMH 2489 (LK18 AHY) is arriving at the 274's Angel terminus on 10 June.

Having tried out one batch of BYD D8UR-DDs, Arriva made the Wrightbus Streetdeck Electroliner its electric double-deck preference in 2023, with the first batch of the resulting ES class going onto the recently regained 307 out of Enfield garage. Coming round the corner at Ponders End on 17 August is ES 12 (LV23 ECW).

With plans firmed up to extend this route through the new Silvertown Tunnel, when it opens, and onward to Beckton, the 129 consolidated its recent extension to Lewisham and traded its 60-reg WVLs for newer vehicles in London Central stock, comprising MCV-bodied Volvo B5LHs displaced from Camberwell by new electric double-deckers. Just having arrived at the new Lewisham station layout on 17 December is New Cross's MHV 12 (BU16 OYW).

Several batches of BYD D8UR electric single-deckers entered service across Go-Ahead's spread of companies in 2023, some batches having to take the place of others as electrification of garages proceeded at different paces. The 366 was won by Blue Triangle from Stagecoach on 29 April and bedded in with SEs (see page 19) into Henley Road garage until its new SEs, like SEe 208 (LB23 PDX) at Beckton on 7 September, arrived.

The arrival of SEes for the 366 allowed its stand-in E20Ds to leave for a second temporary deployment, that of taking back the 265 for London General on 1 July. Swinging into Alton Road on the first day Putney garage had operated the route since losing it to London United in 2002, SE 279 (YX65 RNV) was subsequently replaced on this route by an older batch of SEs displaced from the 276 after 17 September. SEes 220–232 were intended to electrify this route, but Putney garage had not been fitted out for them, even by year's end.

To make room for the input of the 265 on 1 July, Putney garage handed the 337 back to Stockwell after six years. With it went its batch of 11-reg Enviro400s, including E 161 (SN11 BUV) at Richmond on 9 September.

The need for strengthening works to be carried out on Wandsworth Bridge obliged its closure over the summer period, stranding the 28, 295 and C3 on the north bank. Standing in for them for the interim was a clever combination of their routeings known as 728, entrusted to Abellio with the likes of Battersea-based E40D 2422 (SN61 CYC), seen at Clapham Junction on 9 September.

London Buses: Review of 2023

After nearly 37 years as the only example of a with-the-flow peak-hour express route, the X68 was co-opted into the Superloop network on 29 July as new route SL6, retaining the same configuration and the Camberwell-based ADL E40Hs like EH 221 (YX18 KPL), seen at Aldwych on 20 July.

The 145 was retained by Stagecoach East London and began a new contract on 29 April. Its existing 16-reg ADL E40Ds began to be joined by slightly newer E40H hybrids, made spare from a thumping reduction to the 277 in 2022. 12403 (YY66 PHA) thus moved over from Bow to Barking, and on 17 August is seen setting off from Leytonstone.

On the other side of the Central Line from the previous picture, the western example of Leytonstone's pair of small but heavily trafficked bus stations sees the arrival on 17 August of 67011 (YJ23 EWM), one of a dozen new Switch MetroCity EVs ordered by the former Tower Transit for its retention of the 339, but received by Stagecoach East London after the bigger firm took over.

April 2023 saw Arriva London North announced as keeping hold of the 349 with its existing Borismasters for a five-year term, with a contract commencement date of 2 September. However, on 29 July it was reallocated from Edmonton to Enfield garage, and on 17 August near its new base is seen LT 4 (LTZ 1004, ex-LT61 DHT). A number of Borismasters shuffled around between these two garages and Tottenham to fulfil an age requirement concomitant with the contract, but this bus was already based at Enfield and stayed where it was.

Unable to accommodate the BDEs ordered for it, the 204 instead began converting in July to the WDE-class Wrightbus Streetdeck Electroliners intended for the 142. Coming up to its home at Edgware on 19 November is WDE 2773 (LV23 DGZ), demonstrating a change from long-established Metroline practice in that the offside fleetnumber is below the driver's cab, there being no room above where various logos have crowded it out.

An epic round-the-houses trek from Uxbridge to Heathrow that could be accomplished in half the time by express route A10, the U3 out of Metroline West's Uxbridge garage was obliged to hand over its E20Ds to Willesden Junction for the takeover of the H17 on 2 September. In their stead came what members of the 60-reg batch of Enviro400s weren't selected to leave fleet strength at that time, with TE 1099 (LK60 AHJ) demonstrating at Heathrow on 7 September. Plans were floated by year's end to make this route even longer by incorporating the U1 in its entirety.

Confirmed during 2023 as a dead man walking in bus terms, Metrobus's 455 flickered to life in its probable last year of existence when it inherited the S1's Optare MetroCity single-deckers upon that route's reallocation from Croydon to Goat Road at London General on 12 August. Coming through Croydon town centre on the 22nd is OM 4 (YJ14 BFA), new as Quality Line OM 01.

When moved to Goat Road on 12 August, the S1 was converted to a mix of SE and SOE operation, exemplified in this 22 August Sutton town centre shot of SOE 34 (LX09 EVB), of a class otherwise leaving fleet strength in considerable numbers.

Its immediate future cemented by its award to and retention by Arriva London South in December 2022, the 417 began its new contract on 19 August 2023, with new Wrightbus Streetdeck Electroliners ordered. However, on the first day of that contract, it was reallocated from Norwood to Brixton, taking its ex-Dartford Enviro400s with it. Arriving at Clapham Common on 26 October is T 288 (GN61 JPY), new as Arriva Kent Thameside 6458. The 417's new ESs were all in place by the end of the year (see page 41).

New in 1989 but always rather an add-on to the tight-knit network of H-routes in the Harrow locality, the H17 was awarded in 2023 to Metroline, with Willesden Junction garage of the Metroline West company taking over on 2 September with transferred E20Ds like DEL 2265 (LK66 FTF), seen in Harrow on the 5th.

Already resident on the 79, Sovereign's Edgware-based Volvo B5LH VH 45300 (LF18 AYC), seen in Edgware on 5 September, saw its route treated on the 2nd to a useful diversion away from Alperton Sainsbury's to Stonebridge Park. The 83 took over its previous short run onwards from Alperton station.

London Buses: Review of 2023

Having enjoyed repeated periods of double-deck substitution in recent years, it was about time that the 203, busier than it looks, went over to this mode permanently. It had last used them on a full-time basis with RTs prior to one-manning in 1972, but Volvo B5LHs fit in just fine. The last of its Mercedes-Benz Citaros to operate was MCL 30302 (BD11 LWO), seen at Hounslow on 24 August, eight days before its withdrawal.

London United's Scania N230UDs finally dwindled to nothing in August, but two were revived to cover refurbishments to Hounslow's ADEs. Logo-less on 7 September in the town centre is SP 40051 (YT09 BNJ).

Chop and Change

The full horror of 'tomatoing' is even clearer in front of a bright late-summer sun, as Edgware's MMC E20D DEL 2245 (LK66 EOR), just refurbished and transferred in for Metroline's takeover of the 251 on 2 September, is getting under way from Edgware on the 5th. This wasn't the only aesthetic outrage perpetrated in 2023, as two other TfL contractors had mid-life vehicles refurbished with horribly clashing seat materials.

Operated by distant Palmers Green only by virtue of this being the closest Arriva London North garage after Garston closed in 2018, the 340 in the Harrow area struggled and was lost the next time it was tendered. On 2 September it was taken up by Sovereign, based yards from its Edgware terminus, and two strains of Volvo B5LHs were assigned to run it. Coming into Harrow on the 5th of that month is VH 45309 (LF68 PYU), already based at Edgware and familiar on the 79, but others were ex-Tower Transit examples recently spare from London United at Westbourne Park.

Ever stepchildren, not just at their Sovereign home but because they were six of the only eight ever built, the Wrightbus SRM-bodied Volvo B5LHs, superficially resembling Borismasters, found more regular work at Edgware when the 340 was assumed on 2 September; hitherto, they had been wasting their lives as school buses. They could be said to have kicked off the 'ugly' period of refurbishments, having replaced their gold handrails and red seats with fleet colours that jarred against their existing maroon walls. On 29 December VHR 45203 (LJ16 MUV) is inside Harrow bus station.

Needing just three buses to bumble up the steep hill from Coulsdon to the housing estate built over the old asylum at Cane Hill, the 404 changed operators on 30 September, passing from London United, heirs to the old Quality Line, to Abellio. On 14 October, an unexplained massive queue of cars into the ALDI at Coulsdon has caused Beddington Cross-based MMC E20D 8219 (YX16 OBH) nearly to blow the angle needed for a decent shot, with another bus not due for half an hour and a storm brewing.

30 September also saw Metrobus take over the 450 from Arriva London South, replacing its 66-reg Wrightbus Streetlites with new BYD D8UR electrics to the intermediate 9.7m length and therefore just right for this circuitous route. Coming into West Croydon on 14 October is Croydon's SEe 252 (LG73 FYN).

In order to transform existing express route X26 into new Superloop route SL7 on 19 August, Go-Ahead had to strip Blue Triangle's River Road garage of as many WVL-class Volvo B9TLs as it could to match the stock already operating. That meant saddling the 101 with superannuated Enviro400s like E 114 (LX09 FBE), taken off the 57 at Merton and seen at Beckton on 7 September. The 101 was already announced as retained by its incumbent for a 2 March 2024 renewal on the basis of new electric double-deckers, so this situation was felt acceptable in the short term.

Chop and Change

The 276 was just one of a growing number of routes whose bold new generation of electric single-deckers were months off introduction or even delivery. Taken over by Stagecoach East London on 16 September and based at the old Tower Transit garage at Lea Interchange, the route was expecting examples of Volvo's new BZL, but had to get going with ageing Enviro200s recently made spare when their old D3 was lost to Go-Ahead. Leaving Stratford on the first day of operations is 36354 (LX59 AOE). No BZLs were in evidence by year's end.

Introduced in 1999 to accompany the Jubilee Line Extension, the D3 offered links out of the Isle of Dogs peninsula to Wapping and Bethnal Green, with a number of significant structural changes implemented since then. It had only ever been operated by Stagecoach East London, but in 2023 it was won by Blue Triangle and taken over by that Go-Ahead firm on 16 September. At least here, its intended 10.2m BYD D8UR electrics were ready, though the batch exemplified by Henley Road's SEe 201 (LB23 PCX) at Bethnal Green on the first day was actually meant for the 366.

Since 1988 the basic link from Upminster station under the low bridge to Upminster Park Estate, the two-bus 346 passed on tender from Blue Triangle to Stagecoach East London on 30 September. The three E20Ds refurbished for it came from the stocks inherited with the takeover of Tower Transit, and at Upminster station on 2 December, we can just about see, unfortunately, that Rainham's 37581 (YX65 RMY), new as Tower Transit DM 45117, has had its seats reclad in ugly and cheap-looking grey PVC. Plans are at hand to extend this route over the 497 in the future.

Though new Wrightbus Streetdeck Electroliners had been ordered for both the 297 and 83 under new Metroline contracts, their operating garage at Perivale remained obstinately unable to charge the buses. Rather than continue to have the WDEs stack up upon delivery, Metroline diverted them to the 113 at Edgware, and on 5 November at Swiss Cottage, we see WDE 2780 (LV23 DHJ).

Abellio liked the Wrightbus Streetdeck Electroliners it had already deployed to the 111, so placed a second order for the type when the C3 was won from Tower Transit. Keep in mind that this route's debut in 1987 was accomplished with just two Sherpa vans, serving a part of town (Chelsea Harbour) that hadn't been built yet. Subsequently pushed onward to Clapham Junction, the modern route is exemplified there on 24 December by Battersea's 3034 (LV73 FDN). At year's end, an even bigger order was placed that would take holdings to three figures.

Docklands Buses' loss of the 276 to Stagecoach East London on 16 September saw half its fleet of 2011-vintage ADL E20Ds transferred from Silvertown to London General at Putney. There, with that garage's installation of electric chargers not ready and the 265's intended SEes therefore forcibly redeployed, they replaced the unreliable 65-reg variety of SEs that had been holding the fort on it since 1 July. On a pleasant 14 October, SE 146 (YX61 BXO) is setting off from the 265's sylvan turning circle at Tolworth, Red Lion.

Electric buses are a sea change in themselves, with their electronic blinds bringing with them a similar new way of having to adapt existing practices, not least in photography where shutter speeds under 1/125 cause one particular manufacturer's displays to flicker. The autumn advent of Ees onto London Central's 40 at Camberwell offered experimentation to find the perfect aperture at which to snap stationary buses in direct sunlight; Ee 196 (LB23 PGU, *above*) at Holborn Viaduct on 5 November was caught at f16, 1/125, 400ASA. No such worries exist on Arriva's Wrightbus Streetdeck Electroliners, though this shot of Brixton Tramshed-based ES 45 (LV23 ZCO, *below*) on 17 December was taken under overcast conditions at Clapham Common.

On 30 September the 168 was withdrawn. In being since clipping off the 68's top third in 1986, it had enjoyed long years of Grey-Green operation before spending the last decade bouncing between Metroline's Cricklewood and Holloway garages. Latterly, it had operated Borismasters, one of which is LT 645 (LTZ 1645) in this 10 June photo taken at Aldwych.

Replacing the 168 was an extension of the 1 northward from Holborn, with that route's stand at Tottenham Court Road handed over to the 188. The 1 had once been an important northwest-to-southeast carrier but, after having gradually lost its roads west of Marylebone, was treated especially harshly in 1991 by being chopped down to barely more than a shuttle into town from inner south-east London. It could do so much better for its prestige number, and that chance has now come. On 5 November, Camberwell's Volvo B5LH MHV 69 (BV66 LGC) is on the new leg at Chalk Farm.

The 32's reallocation within Metroline on 7 January took it from Edgware garage back to Cricklewood, permitting appearances by Borismasters once again, but it was the withdrawal of the 168 on 30 September that freed enough of them to effect a permanent conversion. Coming into Edgware on 19 November is LT 546 (LTZ 1546), tired-looking and in need of the refurbishment that was beginning to reach its late 2015-vintage batch by then.

Chop and Change

The small Peckham garage of London Central has had to face some tough questions in recent years as, one by one, its core routes have been lost to local competitors, principally Abellio. The 63 had already passed to that company, and its runty offshoot 363 went the same way on 11 November. Here at Peckham Rye on 6 December is Walworth's 2570 (YX17 NVS), one of a number of E40Hs made spare earlier in the year by the hacking down of the 427.

Happily for Peckham, just as many local routes have been awarded to London Central and put into the garage to replace those lost. One such was the 78, between 1954 and 1990 Peckham's bread and butter but only restored on 2 December 2023 with the E40Hs that had had to abandon the 363 four weeks previously. EH 67 (YX66 WHJ) is also at Peckham Rye on 6 December, with the route also seeing MHVs from the remnant still held.

To prepare a home for the return of route 157 to Merton upon London General's win of that route, the 44 was reallocated to Stockwell on 25 November, taking with it the entire WSD class of Wrightbus Streetdeck diesels. Though showing neither garage code nor the new running number series (SW21+) to indicate its move, nor any front logos at all, WSD 13 (SN18 XZG) is short-working to the extraordinarily cramped side-street stand at Tooting Broadway that has to simultaneously accommodate three busy routes over and above occasional curtailments like this.

With Sutton's 151 unable to commence its intended conversion to Ee operation, the 213 took its buses, and that route's own complement arriving later started going onto the 57 at Merton at the end of the year. Just having drawn up to the end of the line at Kingston on Christmas Eve is Ee 180 (LG23 EUX).

The 185's conversion from mixed MHV and EH operation to BYD D8UR-DD electrics under the terms of its retained London Central contract was achieved seamlessly, putting into Camberwell garage new buses like Ee 202 (LG73 FTK). It is captured on 17 December under the glowing roundel surmounting Vauxhall station.

Having started off the electric double-decker era with BYD D8UR-DDs, Stagecoach in London changed its mind, taking not only the fashionable Wrightbus Streetdeck Electroliner but hedging its bets by ordering Volvo BZLs as well. The new buses into Catford garage for the 199 threw up two surprises, first that the blinds were powered rollers that had otherwise ceased to be specified, and second, that they had the TfL interior, similarly long sidelined. On 17 December, a shiny 82007 (LV73 FEJ), finally showing off the group's new fleetnumber font, is on the outskirts of Lewisham.

With London United all but extinguishing Scania N230UD operation, Stagecoach became the last London operator of the type, with a full runout on West Ham's 97 and a handful of stragglers in support on Plumstead's 96. Though the latter, in the person of 15076 (LX09 AFA) at Bluewater on 2 December, are down to single figures, the 97's contract is up first, at which point (2 March 2024) it will be moving to Lea Interchange garage and taking on Volvo B5LHs.

West Croydon is not what it was; in this author's heyday a fine record shop by the name of Mi Price occupied the spot being passed on 17 December by Merton's WVL 434 (LX11 FJO), a Wrightbus Gemini 2-bodied Volvo B9TL transferred from Docklands Buses after the loss of the D7 to stand in on the 157 from the date of its takeover by London General until new electric double-deckers come on stream.

Yet another route whose base is unable to field the electric buses already delivered for it is the W5, renewed by its incumbent Stagecoach East London on 4 February. The Switch MetroCity EVs even shorter than those that assumed control of the 339 at Lea Interchange in the summer were drafted to support this route while Ash Grove powers up. They occupy a fleetnumber range all their own to distinguish their length; this one, seen at Mile End on 29 December, is 45008 (YJ23 EHZ).

A routine contract retention in 2023 was that of the 147, which remained with Blue Triangle at River Road. Despite being specified for existing hybrid double-deckers, its contract, commencing on 6 May, was for the full seven years otherwise only awarded to routes promising electrics. Even so, the hybrids themselves had to be sourced to see off the current 61-reg Enviro400 diesels, and these were seven-year-old Volvo B5LHs (MHVs) made spare from Camberwell's 185. Now settled at River Road in this Ilford shot of 29 December is MHV 9 (BU16 OYS).

It only took 21 months since its takeover from Metroline, but the 235 finally activated its intended fleet of BYD D8UR electrics in October, now that their base at London United's Hounslow Heath had had the juice turned on. Setting off from the sleepy Sunbury Village terminus on 27 December is BE 37080 (LB71 OAH), though the driver would do well to set the blinds for the correct direction before he puts the hammer down.

Having dodged withdrawal after the dread scheme of 2022 was cancelled for the most part, the D7 resumed its place in the tendering queue and was lost by Docklands Buses to Stagecoach East London. On 2 December the new operator took over, using Enviro400s spare from Catford's 199 pending the delivery of an order for the double-deck variant of Volvo's new electric BZL. However, Ash Grove added examples of its existing fleet, in the shape of ex-HCT Group E40H Citys from the 26 and 388. Laying over at the D7's Mile End stand on 29 December is 12534 (SN66 WRX).

The 55's contract renewal of 26 February 2022 had seen its PVR reduced from 38 Borismasters to 34. With nowhere for them to go other than out of Stagecoach East London, the surplus held in place at Leyton and began to drift onto the 215, being newer than the 12-reg E40Ds used hitherto. About to make the simplified turn from Hoe Street into Selborne Road at Walthamstow Central on 29 December is LT 268 (LTZ 1268), transferred from Bow to Leyton on 30 November and with a recent refurbishment given away by non-standard fleetnumber transfers.

Another move born of frustration with the pace of infrastructure electrification saw half a dozen of Metroline's Wrightbus Streetdeck Electroliners not already deployed to the 113 pressed into service on the 317 out of Potters Bar, covering for Optare MetroDecker EV (OME) failings. Disgorging its passengers at the last stop before the stand at Enfield Town, Little Park Gardens, on 29 December is WDE 2862 (LV23 ZBD).

Abellio rounded off the year with a name change to formalise its takeover from Nederlands Railways earlier in the year. Now emblazoned as Transport UK at Clapham Junction on Christmas Eve is ADL E40H 2444 (SK14 CTZ), of the hybrid contingent based at Battersea for the 156 and 345.

Chapter 4

Superloopy, Nuts Are We

It spawned a myriad of nicknames; Stupidloop, Superloopy, even Pooperscoop; but the network of express routes promised by Boris Johnson and finally, albeit hurriedly, put into practice by TfL from mid-2023 has been a success. Even with relatively discreet branding and existing vehicles rather than the suite of electric buses that would really extol the network's green credentials, ridership on the five routes introduced in 2023 has soared. All that stands in their way, really, is the state of traffic, still unbudged even when soaked almost dry by the ULEZ, just the latest in a rash of money-making exercises imposed on people bold enough to be entering London by car. Express services like these represent the distant hope that they won't have to.

The Superloop routes so far are as follows:

Route	Introduced	Formerly	Extent	Operator (Garage)	PVR (Mon–Fri)
SL8	15 July 2023	607	Shepherd's Bush–Uxbridge	Metroline West (**G**)	20 VMH
SL6	29 July 2023	X68	Russell Square–West Croydon	Go-Ahead (**Q**)	10 EH
SL7	19 August 2023	X26	West Croydon–Heathrow	Metrobus (**C**)	20 WVL
SL9	26 August 2023	X140	Heathrow–Harrow	Sovereign (**SO**)	13 BCE
SL10	25 November 2023	New	Harrow–North Finchley	Sovereign (**SO**)	13 BCE
SL1	2 December 2023	New	North Finchley–Walthamstow	Arriva LN (**AD**)	11 HA

2024 will see the debut of routes **SL2** (Walthamstow–North Woolwich), **SL3** (Thamesmead–Bromley) and **SL5** (Bromley–West Croydon), with the **SL4** (Grove Park–Canary Wharf) rounding out the ten in 2025.

Pioneering the Superloop network on 15 July 2023 is the SL8, one of the three routes that don't form a loop. New in 1991, the 607 was a well-received express adjunct to the long 207 along the Uxbridge Road, that had worked hard its three decades' worth of RMs, RMLs, DMs, RMLs again and then Ms. LXs and LSs fitted with coach seats came next, followed in 1995 by Volvo Olympians and in 2000 by Dennis Tridents (TNLs). Volvo B7TLs, later with Enviro400 help, spanned the 2010s before 2019's intake of MCV-bodied Volvo B5LHs like Greenford's VMH 2591 (LF19 FXS), now in Superloop livery at Uxbridge on 24 August.

Able to fly past 207s and 427s, the 607 was nonetheless given even more to do when the latter route was pulled out of two-thirds of its remit on 4 March, in the hope that the Elizabeth line would pick up the slack. Superloop SL8 thus inherited this extra work, with VMH 2571 (LA68 DWV) coming into Ealing on 17 August.

It will be noted that the nearside and offside treatments of Superloop livery don't match, and as will be seen on buses with exposed staircases, the network's rainbow roundel has to be sacrificed. Still, it's simple and to the point, without being particularly adventurous. Leaving Uxbridge on 24 August is VMH 2586 (LF19 FXL).

Even less fitted to Superloop format is the SL6, carried over from with-the-flow peak-hour express route X68, and unfortunately now unable to use its branded buses elsewhere, forcing them wastefully to sit out the day out of use. Camberwell's ADL E40H EH 215 (YX18 KPA) of London Central is leaving Waterloo on 17 August.

Finally given the frequency it demanded, busy half-hourly X26 became SL7 every 15 minutes on 29 August. It now needed 20 buses, with additional Volvo B9TLs having to be transferred to Metrobus's Croydon garage and the incumbents reliveried in turn. Still red at Heathrow on 5 September is WVL 340 (LX59 DDZ).

Similar to the X26's incumbent Volvo B9TLs but still more than a decade old, WVL 490 (LJ61 NWC) was one of a large number of its batch seconded from Blue Triangle to Metrobus for the SL7's inaugural boost, though without the comparable single-door conversion. It is getting going from West Croydon on 22 August.

Now treated to Superloop livery in this Kingston, Wood Street view of 16 September is WVL 342 (LX59 DDA) of the original X26 batch. This bus and its original fellows have been treated specially throughout their lives, having started on the Barking Riverside-exploiting EL-routes and carrying their East London Transit colours.

Relatively new itself and already treated to one operator change, the X140 had established itself as a nippy and useful carrier from Heathrow to Harrow over limited stops once worked by the 140 at its former maximum extent. It now became SL9, retaining its Sovereign Harrow-based BYD D8UR-DD electrics like BCE 47106 (LG71 DVF), seen coming into Hayes town centre on 5 September.

Showing off the rear treatment of the SL9's blue-accented version of Superloop livery at Heathrow on 5 September is BCE 47105 (LG71 DVC), with two of the SL7's Metrobus Volvo B9TLs for comparison.

Sovereign's Harrow garage gained a second Superloop route on 25 November. The SL10 was new, though was planned as X183, as the 183 was the route it shadowed before dipping off to finish at North Finchley. With orange-flavoured branding in this Harrow bus station shot of 27 December is BCE 47115 (LG22 AUC).

X34 was the draft identity for the SL1, introduced by Arriva London North on 2 December with ADL E40H City hybrids just displaced from the 78 at Ash Grove but rushed to Palmers Green in time for reliverying. Having battled treacherous North Circular Road traffic, HA 5 (LK65 BZB) is nearing Arnos Grove on 27 December.

Chapter 5

Advert Buses

With a nod to *London's Advert Buses* by this author, another look is taken at the all-over ad scene. Once again, the numbers of schemes in 2023 alone are almost too huge to count, with at least 300 individual vinyls reported in a range of products, services and pursuits covering entertainment, clothes and shoes, food and drink, technology and communications, banking, energy, events, TfL itself and even a couple of red herrings. As ever, the majority of adverts adorn the characteristic Borismaster, but with a decision to expand adverts to cover the front of electric buses as well, the full spirit of the exercise will be maintained. This account endeavours to cover as many as it can, but can only hint at the extent out there.

Ever corny but just as endearing, Abba continue to eke out their five decades in existence with a new concert based on virtual-reality captures and re-recorded songs. Two of five Borismasters to plug this affair between April and June were LT 965 (LTZ 2165, *left*) of Arriva London South's Norwood garage, seen taking it across Marble Arch on 4 June, and Abellio's Walworth-based LT 779 (LTZ 1779, below) at Aldwych on 27 April. Later in the year, LT 965 was wrapped again, this time for EE Mobile, but LT 779 has returned to red.

One of the Sega Genesis's inaugural games and later to become iconic, *Sonic the Hedgehog* has experienced a revival, with the issue of a new game on multiple platforms. The five characters of *Sonic Superstars* each gained their own bus-side advert in this campaign, with Borismaster LT 857 (LTZ 1857) of London Central's New Cross garage debuting 'Amy Rose' in November. Seen at the Elephant & Castle on 19 November, it had been a busy bus in 2023, already having sported ads for Gant, Marc Jacobs, *Star Wars: Jedi*, Nākd, Top Boy and ELF Cosmetics.

Another franchise with more than a few years behind it, *Teenage Mutant Ninja Turtles* spawned yet another reboot in the form of an animated movie entitled *Teenage Mutant Ninja Turtles: Mutant Mayhem*. Emerging from Baylis Road on 17 August, Arriva London South LT 723 (LTZ 1723) of Brixton garage received the wrap in August with four other Borismasters, undoubtedly helping the film to a positive box-office performance with good reviews. LT 723 had already advertised Battersea Power Station and Tinder before donning this particular ad.

After music, video games and movies, this year's entertainment category concludes with a pro wrestling event mounted by the WWE at the O$_2$ Arena and simultaneously livestreamed on a pay-per-view basis. *Money in The Bank* of 1 July was that body's first British event since 2003, but competitors AEW were beginning to press. Arriving at Walthamstow Central on 17 August is LT 315 (LTZ 1315) of Stagecoach East London's Leyton garage, one of five Borismasters to wear the ad. It was the only ad carried by this particular LT in 2023.

London Buses: Review of 2023

Fashion giant Marc Jacobs' all-over ad for 2023 was imposing and perhaps a little difficult to read, but it adorned seven Borismasters in the first half of the year. So wrapped between February and June is LT 377 (LTZ 1377) of Stagecoach East London's Leyton garage, which had already carried an ad for ITVx. It is seen at Tottenham Court Road on 21 March.

On the new section of the 21 to Holloway rather than Newington Green is LT 872 (LTZ 1872) of London Central's New Cross garage, captured at Highbury Corner on 4 June. It was liveried for Levi's 501s between April and May, but this was only the second of six adverts worn this year, the others being for Tu, *The Full Monty*, Naked Drinks, Asahi and EE Mobile. The four Borismasters already plugging the essential jeans brand came to the end of their run earlier in 2023, but four more were then commissioned and this was one of them.

On 27 April, the last but one day the famous 11 served St Paul's, London General's Stockwell-based LTs 61 (LTZ 1061) and 506 (LTZ 1506) pass. Jennifer Lopez is hardly someone you'd liken to the back end of a bus, but that was what she was commissioned to ride for Intimissimi lingerie between March and May, as part of a four-Borismaster campaign. LT 506 had already plugged Moncler and Hogwarts and would go on to do the same for Tinder and *Teenage Mutant Ninja Turtles: Mutant Mayhem*.

27 April was also the penultimate day of the 332, though under the skin it would continue on the 29th as a revamped 16, this number deemed too prestige to admit being withdrawn in its old format. COS is part of the H&M Group, and in the first part of 2023 launched an ad campaign on ten Borismasters, one of which was Metroline's LT 804 (LTZ 1804) of Cricklewood garage. Treated in March and seen turning off the Edgware Road, it was the last to lose its vinyl in August, by which time six more Borismasters with COS ads were coming on stream.

Occupying either end of the luxury spectrum are Loewe, an LVMH offshoot, and Tu, Sainsbury's cheerful in-house bargain clothing brand. Both meet here astride Borismasters in this Parliament Square shot of 27 April, with LT 854 (LTZ 1854) of London Central's New Cross garage turning right and LT 71 (LTZ 1071) of London United's Shepherd's Bush turning left. Loewe's campaign was on five buses, this representative carrying it between April and May, while Tu sponsored four; LT 71 was so adorned between March and May, with other ads carried by each during the year.

Five years after the last Borismaster rolled off the production lines at Wrightbus, successors have had little of the uniqueness or associated prestige until electric buses, with all their PR advantage, came along. They alone have been allowed to carry all-over ads across the front as well, maximising their potential. About to cross Clapham Junction on 24 December is BYD D8UR-DD BCE 47008 (LB69 JNX) of London United's Shepherd's Bush garage, which was treated at year's end to an ad for Rihanna's Creeper Phatty shoe on her Fenty brand.

Most all-over vinyl wraps are imaginative, lively and follow buses' lines. Some, however, are just horrid. Ovo Energy is unimpeachable enough, but its house colours of ghastly green just make buses so treated look bloodshot around the eyes, as on London General's Merton-based Optare MetroDecker EV Me 17 (YJ21 EYW) at Mitcham on 22 August. Accordingly, the company has only advertised on electric double-deckers, and has done it relentlessly, sponsoring two dozen in 2023. This one was wrapped in December 2022 and was still green a year later.

Every electric double-deck model running in London in 2023 has an OVO representative in the company's lurid green, but by virtue of sheer numbers, the BYD D8UR-DD has most members. Here at Archway on 7 April is BDE 2632 (LJ19 CVF) of Metroline's Holloway garage; within weeks it would be losing this ad after a full year.

Displaying the Optare MetroDecker EV's original front before the mandatory imposition of that awful, goitre-like cowl is Potters Bar garage's OME 2658 (YJ19 HVL) of Metroline, setting off on a typical route 134 journey from North Finchley on 19 November. Its tenure as an OVO billboard has been even longer, the green wrap having been applied as far back as April 2022.

With classic buses in the background serving the Chalk Farm running day (see Chapter 8), LT 20 (LTZ 1020) of Abellio's far-off Battersea garage takes a 24 out of Hampstead Heath on 5 November. British Gas had just sponsored five Borismasters, and this was one of them.

Showing off the 3's new Victoria destination since 28 April is Borismaster LT 711 (LTZ 1711), another Battersea-based Abellio motor but curiously, not blinded for the 24, which came to that garage at a later date. Seen on 17 December at Crystal Palace, it is one of five LTs branded for EE Mobile since the autumn.

Six food and drink advert wraps follow now, headed by Chiquita's playful campaign plugging its own bananas. Six London United BCEs and a single OME participated, each one with a different treatment, and here at Clapham Junction on 25 July is BCE 47016 (LB69 JPJ) of Shepherd's Bush garage.

Nākd offer a range of natural fruit and nut bars, and in 2023 sponsored eight Borismasters. Thus treated to the appropriate vinyl over May and June was LT 761 (LTZ 1761) of Metroline's Holloway garage, and on 4 June it is speeding down Park Lane towards Victoria.

These days, Mentos sweets are perhaps less well known for eating than from the volcanic reaction produced when they are dropped into a bottle of Coke. Perhaps with that in mind, the company has formulated a chewing gum, simultaneously making much of the paper bottles containing it. Arriva London South Borismaster LT 964 (LTZ 2164) of Brixton garage demonstrates at Clapham Common on 17 December, having received this ad the previous month. It had also advertised *Call of Duty* earlier in the year.

Not a Borismaster or electric and thereby qualifying only for a three-quarter ad, Arriva London North's Tottenham-based Volvo B5LH HV 350 (LF67 EUV) is at Holborn Circus on 5 November, having advertised Highland Spring water since July. Just one other bus participated in this modest campaign, London General's WHV 79.

After the kind of traffic Arriva London North's Tottenham-based Borismaster LT 197 (LTZ 1197) had to fight through on 16 September to reach Hyde Park Corner, its passengers would be needing a beer; why not an Asahi, which sponsored this and four other Borismasters in the second half of the year. Once its contract advertising Asahi was up, this bus gained an ad for COS.

Stepping up through the strengths of alcohol being pitched at Londoners, we see Borismaster LT 680 (LTZ 1680) of London United's Stamford Brook taking an ad for Courvoisier round Hyde Park Corner on 16 September. There were five of these, and when this one's four months came to an end shortly after this picture was taken, it stayed on the alcohol theme by donning an ad for Brewdog.

London Buses: Review of 2023

For a long time prior to the resurgence of all-over adverts, only training buses were permitted to carry anything other than their companies' fleet liveries, for fear of confusing passengers. Nowadays, bus driving is an advert in itself, with each firm having to vie for custom in the same way as for tenders. At Hayes & Harlington station on 21 March, Abellio's attractive training livery adorns ADL Enviro400 9422 (LJ07 OPH), otherwise retired from service at the end of 2018.

In June, Abellio's BYD D8UR-DD 3406 (LC71 KWO) of the 63's contingent out of Walworth was treated to a TfL ad with the theme 'Every Story Matters', participating thereafter in official events and taking part in the Imberbus running day that August. Here it is at Holborn Circus on 5 November.

Before the decision was made to spin off the existing express routes as part of the Superloop network, the Volvo B9TLs pounding up and down the X26 for Metrobus at Croydon were given their own wrap, playing up the service's link to Heathrow and the fact that it charged the same £1.75 fare as any other London bus route. Coming into Kingston on 10 June is WVL 336 (LX59 DDO).

Advert Buses

TfL's budget for its own publicity seems bottomless, with a dozen electric buses across several fleets given a scheme extolling their zero-emissions credentials. Coming round Hyde Park Corner on 16 September, this time from the east after the rerouting of the 23 on 28 April, is London Transit's Westbourne Park-based Optare MetroDecker EV OME 46031 (YJ21 EXD).

The mass influx of Ee-class BYD D8UR-DDs onto three Sutton garage-operated routes of London General during 2023 is celebrated by a typical example, Ee 169 (LG23 EZO) at Morden on 10 December. Unusually, with one exception (see below), these ads do not go all around the buses.

Alone among the contingent of 'This bus is zero-emission' TfL wraps, Metroline's brand new WDE 2799 (LV23 DJZ), a Wrightbus Streetdeck Electroliner fresh into service at Edgware garage on the 204, was given an all-over ad, due to its being 'London's 1,000th zero-emission bus'. Seen leaving Edgware on 5 September, it took a break from its established work (which had also begun to include visits to the 113 and 142) to guest on the 221 for the Finchley running day on 19 November (see page 84).

The Coronation of King Charles III on 6 May merited a suite of commemorative liveries. There were four themed colours, two of which are shown here. Above in pink is Abellio 3006 (LV72 BJZ), a Wrightbus Streetdeck Electroliner just into service on the 111 out of Twickenham garage and pictured at Kingston bus station on 11 June, two months before this site closed for reconstruction. Below, in Edgebury, New Eltham, on 4 June is Stagecoach Selkent 84148 (LG71 DNV), one of the 160's BYD D8UR-DDs new to Catford in 2022 but renumbered this year from 14148. The other colours were red (LTs 190 and 511) and cyan (LT 70), with each of the five buses proclaiming 'God Save the King' on the offside and 'Happy & Glorious' on the nearside.

A little on the vague side, the advert on most of London Transit's Westbourne Park-based Volvo B9TL VH 45102 (BD13 OHV) is for Verkada, a provider of cloud-based security systems. Seen on 21 March at Notting Hill Gate, this bus was transferred to Park Royal garage in the second week of May, reverting to all-red at the same time.

Barclays sponsored this year's Wimbledon tennis championships, and one of the six Borismasters so wrapped, LT 745 (LTZ 1745) of Metroline's Holloway garage, is seen on 29 June at King's Cross.

This advert offers the undoubted thrill of being able to get away with using the word 'crap' in a caption! Earthily-named Australian company Who Gives a Crap produces recycled toilet paper, and in 2023 sponsored three electric double-deckers, one of which was Arriva London South BYD D8UR-DD EA 12 (LG71 DKJ) from the 319's allocation at Brixton. However, on 10 June it is seen crossing the Elephant & Castle on the 133, not long before the announcement that this route had been lost to Abellio.

Chapter 6
Odd Workings

Nothing thrills London bus enthusiasts more than sighting on a route a bus that's not supposed to be there. Though vehicles are much more varied than in London Transport days, they are still allocated by type to a specific route, increasingly according to contract specifications. Even so, any TfL operator's typical garage has several other routes to maintain at once, and with the maxim that any bus is better than no bus, is perfectly at will to substitute another route's buses if needed. Here are examples of what could be found off-piste over 2023.

Metrobus's 353, operated out of the company's original Orpington garage, had only relatively recently upgraded from Scania to Enviro400 (E) operation, but its retained contract applying from 22 September 2022 specified new electric double-deckers, as and when they were delivered (and the garage equipped to charge them). The resulting Ee-class BYD D8UR-DDs went into service from 18 March 2023, but from time to time hybrid E40Hs from the 208 would stray over, as EH 314 (YW19 VPF) is doing in Orpington High Street on 21 March.

Operated since 2019 with Optare MetroDecker EVs (OMEs), the 134 from Metroline's Potters Bar garage often had to see hybrid double-deckers substituted, on one alarming occasion *en masse* when two OMEs were destroyed in a battery fire. No more were ordered, Metroline instead turning to Wrightbus's new Streetdeck Electroliner. The prototype, WDE 2769 (LV22 AGX), was put into service on 9 February, and on 27 April is seen at Archway.

The pitiable remnants of the 72 dodged outright withdrawal, but that meant that its existing contract had to be sorted out. It was announced as retained by its incumbent, London United, in March 2023, but on the basis of diesel buses. With the 235 unable as yet to convert to the new electrics already delivered for it, the BEs were switched to Shepherd's Bush garage and began turning out on the 72, as in this shot of BE 37098 (LG72 EDR) taken on 20 July. Its ageing 59-reg Enviro200s (DEs) were eventually replaced, but by 16-reg DLEs displaced from the 265 after 1 July.

Go-Ahead continued its heavy intake of BYD D8UR electric single-deckers during 2023, taking three lengths but classifying them all as SEes. Those into London General's Merton garage for the 163 and 164 in the spring soon began to visit the 219, otherwise the province of 13-reg Wrightbus Streetlites (WSs). Setting off from Clapham Junction on 9 September is SEe 176 (LG23 FJX).

Confusingly, the chassis from which the SEe derives is also capable of carrying a double-deck body, though with only a DD appellation. Go-Ahead's intake of these, under the Ee class, crossed 200 units in 2023, and two batches were for the 40 and 185 at Camberwell garage of London Central. From the outset, these visited the 35, which fielded a mix of seven-year-old Volvo B5LHs (MHVs) and ADL E40Hs (EHs). Arriving at the 35's Clapham Junction terminus on 24 December is Ee 200 (LB23 PGZ).

London Buses: Review of 2023

Go-Ahead's second batch of Ee-class BYD D8UR-DDs took over the 69 in 2021, operating out of a new site at Henley Road, Silvertown. In 2022, this garage was switched within the group from Docklands Buses to Blue Triangle, permitting a loose pool with the buses of its parent garage at River Road, whose forced reduction in size had made Henley Road necessary in the first place. Thus could WHV-class Volvo B5LH hybrids turn out in support, and not in penny numbers either. At Stratford, WHV 65 (BF65 WJN) is one of three out on 16 September 2023.

It is as rare for Borismaster-operated routes to see substitutions as it is for these buses to stray off their own assigned services. Sometimes, however, any bus is better than no bus, so on 21 March 2023 Stagecoach East London's Bow garage has seconded three ADL E40Ds from the 25 and put them into action on the 8. 11381 (SK20 BBU) is passing through Holborn on its way east.

Despite being a six-mile drive from the Ealing Broadway terminus of the E1 (only three miles long itself), London United's Hounslow garage had its bid accepted and took over the route from Abellio on 29 May 2021. Almost straight away, its ADH-class E40H hybrids were bulked out by the still large number of all-Polish Scania N230UDs based on the H32 and H98. This continued throughout 2023, even after Hounslow's SP fleet was reduced to just two representatives. Coming onto stand on 14 January is SP 40197 (YR10 FGD), which was withdrawn in June.

London United took over the 117 on 4 September 2021 with nine Mercedes-Benz Citaro Ks repurposed from defunct former fellow RATP-group company Quality Line, but the route needs ten buses, so Hounslow's Enviro200s and newer E20Ds assisted from the beginning. Coming into Hounslow town centre on a sunny 7 September is Enviro200 DE 20108 (SN10 CCU).

Not so much an odd working but an initially odd sub-type of bus on the 220, Volvo B5LH VH 45107 (BD13 OJA) was transferred in March with several members of its originally Sovereign batch from Westbourne Park to Park Royal garage, allowing a number of slightly older E40Ds (ADEs) to leave London United fleet strength. On 22 August it is deep in the Wandsworth one-way maelstrom.

Metroline's closure of King's Cross garage on 10 June saw the 30 and 274 reallocated to Holloway with their combined fleet of VMH-class Volvo B5LHs. The garages had always operated an informal pool of vehicles that allowed Holloway's own VWHs to visit, but this was now formalised. On the first day of Holloway operation, VWH 2337 (LK17 DAO) is between St Pancras and Euston stations.

Even before a second major rerouting in five years, the 23's PVR was massively gutted in frequency, freeing a third of its former runout to move over to the 28. At the same time, the route's operator, Tower Transit, changed hands, RATP instituting a new fleetname (or combination of them, reflecting the majority ownership of this ultimately short-lived joint venture) and new fleetnumbers. On 21 March 2023 Optare MetroDecker EV OME 46006 (YJ70 EVH, *above*) is at Notting Hill Gate. Westbourne Park garage's recently added 295 was simultaneously allowing its BYD D8UR-DDs to wander, with BCE 47087 (LG71 DWA, *below*) espied across the road on the same day. This bus later moved to Sovereign Harrow for Superloop route SL10.

Only ever really an adjunct to the main-line Clapham Road route 155, the 355 nonetheless added links at either end, but was prone to being passed about as garage capacity fluctuated. When run by Metrobus at Croydon, its WS-class Wrightbus Streetlites could not rouse themselves in sufficient strength to operate the whole route, so on 7 April at Tooting Broadway WHV 167 (BV66 VLR, *above*) is one of six Volvo B5LHs substituting. On 30 September the 355 was reallocated to London Central at Camberwell to free space for the 1, but the new garage had to offer reinforcements out of its own stocks, thus permitting first-time MHV operation. Here at Tooting (Mitre) on Christmas Eve is MHV 11 (BU16 OYV, *below*), one of three out that day.

Chapter 7

On Their Way Out

All good things come to an end, and usually quicker if they're leased. Leaving the capital in 2023 were further examples of the 2000s generation of ADL Enviro200s, Volvo B9TLs and Scania N230UDs after their statutory decade and a half, with their single-deck counterparts lasting about as long themselves.

A hell of a run was got out of the 318's 57-reg contingent of Mini Enviro200s, half of them indigenous to Arriva London North and the rest acquired from Arriva Kent Thameside. There was simply nothing available to replace buses like Tottenham-based EN 12 (LJ57 UTE), seen at Seven Sisters on 3 June, and even after 9.75m ENRs took over that summer, two had to stay put! This one finished on 3 August but is still in stock.

Scanias as a whole will be history in London once the fleets of London United and Stagecoach finish. The former disposed of all but two in 2023; Hounslow's SP 40043 (YT09 BMU), seen west of the town centre on 4 February, was withdrawn after the H32 passed to Abellio on 4 March and was sold in June.

Seen in Romford on 25 March, Wrightbus Gemini 2 Integral DW 405 (LJ11 AET) of Arriva London North's Grays garage last worked on 28 April. At barely 12 years of age, it represented a bargain for its next owner, Vision Bus of Bolton.

Though the eclectic DOE class was decimated in 2023, all three London General VEs also breathed their last. These very rare combinations of Volvo B9TL chassis with ADL Enviro400 bodywork left Sutton garage at the beginning of the year, but two of them passed to Merton for three more months. On 7 April, VE 2 (LX58 CWL) is bending the corner at Tooting Broadway, not managing to offer any front destination blinds for this particular outing on the 57. It last worked on 4 May and was sold with its siblings to to the provincial operation of Metrobus.

Routine withdrawals of Metroline Enviro400s duly reached the 2009 vintage of the TE class, and TE 939 (LK58 KHD), resident all its life at Potters Bar garage, was withdrawn after 7 February. On 26 January it is seen heading south through Archway.

Chapter 8

Running Days

Increasingly cherished by enthusiasts and, heartwarmingly, by regular Londoners, the classic running day goes from strength to strength. With TfL never particularly strong on PR exercises independent of its own internal publicity, it has fallen to enthusiasts and museums to warm hearts in its stead. Several splendid running days took place in 2023, and covered here are the following:

25 March	Romford	Routes 174 and 175
11 June	Kingston	Routes 65 and 71
16 September	Central London	Route 38
5 November	Chalk Farm	Roures 24, 29, 31, 68, 74 and 139
19 November	North Finchley	Routes 13, 125, 134, 221 and 263
17 December	Bromley	Routes '94' and 227

Also featured are the London Bus Museum's yearly Open Day at Brooklands (16 April) and Ensignbus's running day held on 2 December.

One of the much-loved RLH class of Metro-Cammell-bodied low-height AEC Regents, RLH 53 (MXX 253) served at Harrow Weald (1952–58) and Dalston (1958–70) while a red LT bus, and then spent the next 40 years in the USA. In 2012 it came back to the UK and this year returned to service under the aegis of the London Bus Museum. It is seen at Romford station.

Also a repatriate from abroad, RT 4548 (OLD 768) spent its exile years in Canada; it is now owned by the London Bus Company, which has restored its Abegweit Sightseeing Tours livery.

An extraordinary 85 years old, Chiswick-bodied AEC Regent STL 2377 (EGO 426), owned by the London Bus Museum at Brooklands, boasts sprightlier performance than most modern buses! It is coming round the 175's current terminus at Kent Road, Dagenham, though the route historically continued on to the once-extensive Ford plant to be found by the river.

More recently, preservationists have been tackling the hitherto neglected post-London Transport period. One of the better independents in a sea of mediocrity at that time was Capital Citybus, which enjoyed a varied ordering policy that brought in numerous oddities. A typical one-off is Leyland Olympian 250 (J135 PVC), which had an experimental front that was quickly replaced. After a decade's service in east and north London, it was preserved and its initial front rebuilt from plans. In the company's bright yellow livery, it is passing through Dagenham Heathway.

Interested guests are often welcome on running days, bringing rolling examples of other cities' bus culture. Reading Buses, only 40 miles from London, has long enjoyed a quality scene with a variety of high-spec buses like East Lancs Omnidekka-bodied Scania N94UD 801 (X100 RDG, ex-YN54 AEP), seen at Romford station. Putting to shame the stingy seated capacity of TfL-spec low-floor double-deckers, this beast, even on two axles, seats 90!

London Buses: Review of 2023

Fifty years separate these two London buses seen meeting at Romford station. The London Bus Company's Park Royal-bodied RTL 1105 (LUC 315) is one of Leyland's 1,631-strong answer to AEC's RT and served from 1951 to 1967. DML 41424 (LN51 DXH), meanwhile, is a Marshall Capital-bodied Dennis Dart SLF new to First in 2002 and turned into a trainer in 2010.

An increasingly regular fixture on the rally circuit, AEC Routemaster RML 2579 (JJD 579D) on the approaches to Romford station was new in 1966. It last worked in London service on 26 March 2004, the last day of crew operation on routes 6 and 98 from Metroline's Willesden garage.

Wearing perhaps the most magnificent livery ever to adorn a modern London bus, Leyland Titan T 66 (WYV 66T) is actually on its second go-around in these colours, which were applied in 1983 for London Transport's Golden Jubilee. Much later, long after LT itself had gone, it completed a healthy 21-year service career, finishing at the start of 2001 at what by then was Stagecoach Selkent. Its partner in London General-inspired colours, MCW Metrobus M 57, was also restored to this scheme in its early preservation years but sadly, subsequently lost it.

Only recently accepted as legitimate contenders for rally and running day use, the Dennis Dart in its numerous forms has earned its glory; the type saved the British bus industry when deregulation had otherwise nearly wiped it out. London Buses Ltd was early to the Dart's potential, especially at its initial 8.5m length, which counted as a minibus with the attendant savings on staff wages. 168 DTs with Carlyle bodywork were taken in 1990–91, and two at Brooklands on 16 April are Airbus Direct-spec DT 16 (G516 VYE) and Roundabout-logoed DT 29 (G29 TGW).

Not actually a bus as such, this forward section of an Optare Metrorider was donated by the manufacturer to the London Transport Museum to serve as a fun installation for kids to practise driving a bus; this role had previously been the privilege of what was left of Daimler Fleetline DM 963. A later reclaimed segment replaced it in the LT Museum in due time, in the shape of the section of East Thames Buses Volvo B7TL VWL 5 left undamaged by its arsonists, and the Metrorider passed to the London Bus Museum at Brooklands.

With so many thousands of RT-family buses, interest in where they went after their London Transport stint was just as high as when they were working in the capital. After a service period spanning 1949–66, Park Royal-bodied Leyland RTL 326 (KGU 284) has been through a number of hands since, at one point residing on Jersey. Barton Transport was not one of its subsequent owners, though two dozen RTLs did serve with that historic East Midlands operator and this bus has been restored to mimic them.

London Buses: Review of 2023

Giving unglamorous but stalwart service to London between 1978 and 2004, the MCW Metrobus of 1,485 London members has dwindled to penny numbers two decades after their exit from the front lines, but the survivors continue to feature heavily on running days. That centred on Kingston-area routes 65 and 71 on 11 June saw M 6 (WYW 6T) brought out of its stand at the London Bus Museum and put into service again. Having been based at Norbiton at one point, it will have worked the 65, right at the time its buses carried blinds with all the via points south of Kingston removed.

Keeping on the guest theme in this shot taken round the eastern corner of the Kingston one-way system on 11 June is 1972-vintage Leyland National HOR 416L, of a large batch operated by Provincial. It recalls a similar sight in this part of town and points south over the same period, as fellow NBC company London Country was also obliged to adopt this uninspiring leaf-green livery, with its own fleet of Leyland Nationals comprising the largest fleet of that type.

A much more handsome shade of green was the Lincoln green worn by London Transport's Country Area buses up to, and for a few years after this unit became London Country in 1970. When the first four AEC Routemasters were evaluated in the second half of the 1950s, only RM 2 (SLT 57) saw Country Area service, and very briefly at that. However, since it was based on the 406 out of Reigate, it will have occupied the same spot at Kingston as in this shot, albeit prior to the town centre's chaotic late-1980s reconstruction. The bus station here was itself demolished in the autumn.

The only disadvantage of the modern running day is the pernicious ULEZ, an invisible but psychologically critical barrier separating non-Londoners from their money. In the case of the 65 and 71, newer preserved buses not compliant with the standards could only replicate the routes' historical southernmost section between Chessington Zoo and Leatherhead, long since abandoned but surprisingly still served by TfL buses in the form of today's route 465. Routemaster RM 188 (VLT 188) is turning at today's Chessington World of Adventures complex.

A particularly splendid guest on 11 June was POU 494, a Leyland PD2 new in 1956 to King Alfred of Winchester. After a 16-year career, it was exported to the USA to masquerade as a red 'London' bus but was repatriated in 1999. The Friends of King Alfred Buses continue to hold their famous New Year's Day bus rally in Winchester.

The postwar London Transport buses were almost *too* good; nothing built after the Routemasters could hold a candle to the simplicity and reliability of the capital's purpose-built buses, but the originals could not outrun old age and had to be withdrawn eventually. Taken to replace the quarter-century-old survivors of the bulletproof RF class came 95 Bristol LHs in 1976. BL 88 (OJD 88R, ex-OJD 93R, ex-OJD 88R) was based at Kingston garage in its early years, and in preservation has managed to regain its original registration after co-opting that of a sibling.

On 16 September came an event centred on the 38 alone. Though numerous RTs and Routemasters turned out, they had to contend with scenes like this. Nobody is even supervising a mess of construction barriers blocking the throughput of buses like RM 1005 (5 CLT, ex-ALC 290A, ex-5 CLT) along Piccadilly. This Routemaster is best known for being the last on the 13 on 21 October 2005, and later, in the subsequent ownership of Sir Peter (now Lord) Hendy, has been fitted with a Euro 6 Cummins engine, so it could meet ULEZ restrictions if its age didn't already merit a waiver.

A little further up Piccadilly is RM 1527 (527 CLT, ex-KGW 483A, ex-527 CLT). Though lasting all the way to 2003 in service, when its days assisting on Upton Park garage's 15 came to an end, most of its latter years were spent as a trainer, with the odd secondment to the BBC to serve as a prop on *EastEnders*.

With its conductor, a well-known figure on the circuit, winding the side blinds for another journey out of Victoria and soon to inform the driver that he should be doing the same for the direction he is heading, is RM 2208 (CUV 208C). In 1979, this Routemaster carried Shillibeer livery to celebrate 150 years since horse buses first ran in London, and was still carrying that body by the time it was treated to the livery again, some years after its 1987 withdrawal. However, as can be seen, it is red once again.

Looking resplendent as it descends past Chalk Farm station on 5 November is XF 1 (CUV 51C), one of the two survivors of eight Park Royal-bodied Daimler Fleetlines bought by London Transport in 1965 when it needed to be decided what to specify for the coming era of one-man operation. The XFs bested 50 Leyland Atlanteans in trials and spawned 2,646 DMS-family Fleetlines in the 1970s, but passed to London Country and worked until 1981. This livery is an interim version that preceded the mandatory imposition of NBC leaf green.

In flawless original condition with correct air intakes, numberplates and single nearside foglight, RM 1962 (ALD 962B) is given away only when the roar of its latter-day Scania engine thunders towards you. New in 1964, this bonnet number served for 40 years, coming off with the OPO conversion of the 12 on 6 November 2004. In this shot it is re-creating the former northernmost extent of the 68, which was otherwise pulled back to Euston on 25 October 1986.

Already vulnerable due to its small size and famously militant workforce, Chalk Farm garage was not helped when each of its bread-and-butter routes fell to competitors in the brutal early years of route tendering; the 24 was lost to Grey-Green at the end of 1988, and the 29, most of which was transferred in to take its place, was consolidated with Leaside Buses alone in 1992. If just to keep Chalk Farm alive, new RM-operated route 139 was then introduced, carved out of the northern end of the 159, and it is this era that RM 545 (WLT 545) is recalling while laying over at Camden.

RM 29 (OYM 453A, ex-VLT 29) was one of the 139's inaugural Routemasters into Chalk Farm upon its introduction in 1992. Transferred the next year to Holloway garage, and from late 1994 falling under MTL London Northern's ownership, it continued until the route's one-manning on 28 March 1998. In the TfL era it was bought back and spent 2002–05 in service again, finishing with the last Routemasters of all on the 159 on 9 December 2005. Today, after leaving Camden ahead of RT 1705 (KYY 532), it will pick up the 139 route at Swiss Cottage and carry on to Golders Green.

Star of the Chalk Farm running day was Leyland Titan T 567 (NUW 567Y), also a one-time resident of the eponymous garage and indeed spending the last six and a half years of its scandalously short (1982–93) career there. Its paint job (including early-1990s red entrance doors) was still in decent nick, three decades after the bus was consigned to the reserve collection of the London Transport Museum, and only recently has it been readied for use again. It is seen setting off from Hampstead Heath; then, now and always the 24's northern terminus.

The 31 was one of Chalk Farm's historical staples, and only in 1978 did the garage's participation cease, though Sunday OPO in 1987 brought back an allocation (with Titans) until the ignominious turning over of the whole route to minibuses in 1989. RML operation, as evoked by permanent Metroline preservation piece RML 903 (WLT 903) at Swiss Cottage is also authentic, although the longer Routemasters only operated thus on Sundays during 1974, when enough were spare from the 24.

Silver twice and gold once, RM 1650 (650 DYE) has been in those colours, plus those of Blackpool Transport and Reading Buses, longer than it has in LT red! On 19 November it was one of the numerous classics to turn out in commemoration of the closure by London Buses Ltd of Finchley garage on 4 December 1993. The area is still without a local bus garage and sorely needs one, with local buses having to slog across the border all the way from Potters Bar. The 13, meanwhile, has regained North Finchley as a terminus, though purists will note that it is actually the 82 renumbered.

Though its impact was diluted by being spread across several companies, the Dennis Trident boasted more than 2,000 units new between 1999 and 2006 and only in 2019 did the last examples leave service. Their contribution has been honoured by preservationists, with Alexander ALX400-bodied 18453 (LX05 LLO) a fine example of the type's later production. New in 2005 to Stagecoach East London, it spent most of its life at North Street and last ran on 14 October 2018. Rostered here on the 263, it is showing off the marker lights fitted within the bumper when it was refurbished.

Back on the scene after some time away is RT 4275 (NLE 939), nominally of 1953 vintage but latterly fitted with an earlier Park Royal body than the one with which it entered service. In this shot taken just past North Finchley, it is reprising the period between 1960 and 1963 when it served at Muswell Hill garage. An accident put an end to that spell, but it enjoyed better luck today.

A year out of service after splitting its Arriva career between Palmers Green (2008–19) and Thornton Heath (2019–22), ADL Enviro400 T 8 (LJ08 CVZ) is picking up a route 263 journey from North Finchley. RTL 453 (KLB 548) beside it had a longer career under London Transport, spanning 1948–68, but its late-stage overhaul with a roofbox body brought it distinctiveness that it took into preservation.

Something ultra-modern now, thanks to a local operator. Even then there is historical precedent, as Edgware garage, holders of Wrightbus Streetdeck Electroliner WDE 2799 (LV23 DJZ) under today's Metroline, had a small allocation on the 221 for a year between 21 June 1986 and 6 June 1987. Normally to be found on the 204, this bus has been given an all-over ad billing it as 'London's 1,000th zero-emission bus'.

Eyebrows were raised when the 17, descendant since 1985 of tram-replacement route 104, had its northern section beyond Archway to North Finchley withdrawn in 1991, severing a link across this junction that wouldn't be restored for many years. Former Airbus MCW Metrobus M 1014 (A714 THV), new in 1984, is re-creating a portion of this section when encountered at East Finchley.

Ensignbus's beloved Christmas running day continued even after the Newman family retired. Thus did the usual pantheon of buses from distant and nearer past appear on routes X21, X54, X55 and X81, spanning both sides of the Thames at its greatest width. Lakeside was the focus for the northern bank, here seeing the departure of MCW Metropolitan-bodied Scania BR111DH MD 60 (KJD 260P), the only roadworthy survivor of this short-lived class of 164 buses new in 1976/77.

The single-deck X21 between Upminster and Brentwood saw a fascinating debut in the form of preserved Maidstone & District 2816 (OKO 816G), a Willowbrook-bodied Leyland Leopard new in 1968. Seen breasting the bridge over Upminster station, it was less easily photographed once it had reached Brentwood, as freezing fog had descended! Thankfully, the bus was lovely and warm inside.

Rounding off 2023's rally season was a twin endeavour based on Bromley on 17 December. Not only was the two decades that the 227 spent under RF operation faithfully replicated, but the 94, for many years the key trunk route in south-east London before its abrupt withdrawal in 1982, appeared again for a day. Seen on the edges of Bromley at midday is RF 486 (MLL 463), which, despite serving at a host of garages between 1953 and 1973, wasn't ever one of Bromley's. Its offside foglight is not canon but characteristic nonetheless.

Chapter 9

Tour Buses

Stately and staid in their operation, the tour buses plying a leisurely figure of eight round a host of London's tourist traps and scenic architecture sometimes come to life with a burst of acquisitory activity when companies buy and sell various operators, or new undertakings attempt to compete themselves. 2023 was more eventful than usual, with a couple of unusual services and one new contender for the very deep wallets expected to be emptied on this prestigious work.

Its service period spanning 1959–85, this Routemaster was open-topped for tour work in 1986 and has remained busy in that role, though since with an extra bay and a re-registration that turned it into ERM 84 (JSJ 748, ex-VLT 84), Most recently brought back to the capital after a decade and a half in Edinburgh, this bus now operates with Ghost Bus Tours on its Classic Tour, and on 27 April 2023 it is coming into Parliament Square.

As freakish in nature as the *Harry Potter* Knight Bus from which it takes its inspiration is Golden Tours' 205 (LF20 AXD), a tri-axle Volvo B8TL with MCV EvoSeti bodywork. On 4 June 2023 in Park Lane it is coming back to Victoria from Leavesden Studios.

Tour Buses

You wouldn't expect to be conducted on a grand tour of London in a 14-year-old Enviro200 single-decker, but two such spare Stagecoach East London buses found themselves put to use on the Green Shuttle, an adjunct to CitySightseeing's Red Route that brought potential custom from hotels in Bloomsbury. Thus is West Ham's 36369 (LX59 ECZ) negotiating the new Aldwych configuration on 10 June.

A new entrant to London tour work in 2023 was New York-based Top View Sightseeing, whose livery skewed to the pinker end of red but took advantage of the ability of printed vinyl to showcase some of the capital's usual attractions. Thus done up in this Tower Hill shot of 5 November is 412 (YT09 BJX), an all-Polish Scania N230UD recently sold by London United, with which it had been known as SP 40066. Top View also took on 12-reg E40D double-deckers.

With the sidelining of the 11 and a false start on its own A, Londoner Buses reconfigured its Routemaster-operated stopping service into new route T15, billing it as a competitor to the tour operators and thus enjoying much greater success. Though coming on line of route from the A's old Waterloo stand, the route mimicked TfL's old 15H heritage service and expanded it to Piccadilly Circus, without being hamstrung by the need to shadow an existing stage route. Setting off from Tower Hill on the afternoon of 5 November is RML 887 (202 UXJ, ex-WLT 887).

Chapter 10
On the Fringes

As mentioned last year, outside London is another world altogether, though the £2 single fare recently introduced by central government has provided a much-needed boost to participating local operators who might otherwise have had to resort to demand-responsive vans. At the same time, larger corporates operating staff shuttles from nearby stations have invested in proper buses, increasingly electric for that much-needed PR. Here is a handful of what can be found on the edges of London in 2023, with just as much change and interest as can be encountered in the capital.

The announcement of the sale of Ensignbus by the Newman family to FirstGroup of all people came as a shock, but the company was placed in trustworthy hands and the new patron resolved to remain hands-off. Even so, the 'Top Independent Operator' placard surmounting the fleetname on Wrightbus Streetdeck 177 (LX71 AOM, *above*) in this Lakeside shot of 25 March would have to go. There was still cause for celebration, however, with the treatment of Volvo B9TL 130 (LX15 GPY, *below*) to the X80's original green livery to mark this route's first 20 years. It is also at Lakeside, but during the running day of 2 December.

The outrage over the severing of Potters Bar from Barnet prompted Hertfordshire County Council to work with interested operators on a limited-scope link that was finally realised in 2023 as new route 84B. Serving both Barnet Station and Barnet Hospital in what ultimately became, for reliability purposes, a unidirectional loop, is Central Connect's E20D 330 (CE71 GAL), on its way back to Potters Bar (disregard the unchanged blinds!) at Barnet Church on 29 December.

Now fully integrated with Brighton & Hove under Go-Ahead, Metrobus's extra-London operations both took buses from and supplied them to its parent. Working route 420 southwards out of Sutton on 25 April is 6905 (BJ63 UJN), a Wrightbus Gemini 2-bodied Volvo B9TL new as Brighton & Hove 484.

First Beeline's busy links out of Heathrow to Slough were double-decked in 2023, replacing their decade-old Volvo 7900 hybrids with ADL E40Ds like former First Glasgow 34387 (SK19 EMV), seen leaving the airport's Central Bus Station on 5 September.

London Buses: Review of 2023

Although in a powerful enough position to take over Ensignbus, First Eastern Counties was as moribund as any of the big groups' operations, with elderly vehicles stretched to their limit and less money at hand for things like new liveries. All the same, it was worth commemorating the company's long-gone NBC precursor with the treatment of Enviro400 33424 (VT59 JPT) to Eastern National livery. It is seen on 2 December at Lakeside, having dragged much of the dirt from Basildon with it!

Arriva Southern Counties was similarly suffering hard times, though Deutsche Bahn's long-drawn-out sale of the group to a US hedge fund finally went through in 2023. The Fastrack pair of routes had been partially revitalised with ADL E20Ds including 4127 (SN67 WUT), seen at Greenhithe on 2 December, but the network was tendered and lost to Go-Ahead, which will be putting new Irizar ie trams on it in 2024.

The nadir of bus operation in the modern era is the demand-responsive minibus, commissioned when stage services to isolated areas are just too expensive to put on. Just having come into Bluewater on 2 December is Arriva Kent Thameside's 1033 (RF68 FLP), an EVM Cityline-bodied 15-seat Mercedes-Benz 516CDi Sprinter.

Almost forgotten by enthusiasts is the Dial-a-Ride network, an analogue precursor to the demand-responsive apps of today. Its Volkswagen vans continue to potter around the capital in surprisingly large numbers, and one of the 90-strong Tucana intake of 2018 is Mellor-bodied D 8040 (ML68 JZN), seen in Kingston town centre on 25 April.

In more recent times, large companies' contracted staff services have phased in 'proper' buses rather than vans. In the case of Cobra Corporate Services, its network for Sky now uses Alexander ALX200-bodied BYD D8UR electrics similar to those found on regular bus routes. Accordingly wrapped for Sky is LG22 BOF, seen approaching Ealing Broadway on 17 August.

Just into traffic as 2023 winds down are four new Yutong E10s operated for BP by Passenger Plus. Seen at Feltham station on 27 December is YD73 FRU, about to take staff to the International Centre of Business and Technology (ICBT) in Sunbury; the irony of a petroleum company using electric vehicles is not lost!

It's not much of a Green Line livery when compared to the efforts of old, but Arriva alone retained the trademark after the dust had cleared from the sale, resale and sale again of the former London Country companies. A little old nonetheless to be carrying such a prestige name around Uxbridge on 24 August is Arriva the Shires' Harlow-based 3771 (FL63 DXB), a VDL SB200 with Wrightbus Pulsar bodywork.

The shocking green being propelled into Walton-on-Thames on 14 September by Falcon Buses's MMC E20D YX17 NZA was the livery of Welsh operator Townlynx, from which it had just been acquired. It was quickly repainted in fleet white, red and blue.

Another Falcon acquisition having to use its previous owner's livery is E20D YX12 DLD, new to Abellio as 8777 but recently displaced from the 433 by new Toyota electrics. It is seen on 23 November at the Walton-on-Thames end of the most useful but equally infrequent round-the-houses 400 route.

Surrey County Council route tendering in 2023 took the 458 out of the hands of Diamond Buses (South East) in favour of White Bus, a century-old small operator based in Winkfield. This company had been increasing its profile and did so in spades with the win of this route, plus the 437 ex-Falcon. On 3 September, one of its existing ex-ADL Stock E20Ds, 64 (YY69 TLV, *above*) is captured from a handy berm in New Zealand Avenue, Walton-on-Thames, while a couple of hundred yards back on 18 November is 78 (BV73 MKF, *below*), one of the new permanent complement for the 458 and existing 446. It is one of eight Volvo B8RLEs with MCV EvoRa bodywork, which before the green squares were applied ran about for a few weeks in allover white.

Chapter 11
Looking Ahead

Frustratingly, three new chassis models with examples already delivered, many of them for some considerable time, have not entered service in 2023 due to contractors' inability to power up their operating garages or complete opportunity-charging gantries in time for their routes' contract commencement dates. When they do get going, however, the Volvo BZL, Wrightbus GB Kite Electroliner and Irizar IE Tram will not only advance the percentage of electric buses in London past the 10 per cent already announced with a flourish, but throw their manufacturers' hat in the ring against Alexander Dennis, which is gradually weaning itself off its dependence on China with the belated unveiling this year of the Enviro400EV double-decker and Enviro100EV single-decker.

Until then, as always, many contract changes will be set in motion with existing buses made spare from conversions elsewhere. Here are a few of the changes scheduled for the first part of 2024.

The 9, heavily reduced in the post-COVID era and now the only carrier into the West End from points west, will be retaining Borismasters when it transfers from London United to Metroline on 27 January 2024. Its existing LTs will thus move across with it, seing that all are owned by TfL and dispensed between contractors as necessary. Stamford Brook's LT 462 (LTZ 1462), seen in Piccadilly on 16 September 2023, was new to Stagecoach but came to London United in 2021. Nobody has seen fit to comment that the run-in from the intended operating garage at Brentford is as long as the route itself.

New in 2003 as part of the Congestion Charge expansion pack, the 333 spent its first two contracts with London General at Stockwell before passing to Arriva London South in 2017. From 20 January 2024 it will return to its original garage as a London General win. In its waning days operated out of Brixton, however, its usual mix of ADL E40H Citys (HAs) and Volvo B5LHs (HVs) has been joined by newer examples of the latter transferred in from elsewhere. Leaving Tooting Broadway on Christmas Eve is HV 322 (LK17 AJY), its blinds midway through scrolling alphabetically towards Elephant & Castle.

Famously done out of their intended complement of new buses in 2017 when the DEL-class E20Ds ordered proved to be too long, the 187 and 487 pair had to soldier on with their existing ex-First Enviro200s, like Willesden Junction's DE 1631 (YX58 CPT), looking all of its 15 years of age when encountered at Swiss Cottage on 5 November 2023. When the infrastructure is ready, these routes will become Metroline's inaugural pitch for Volvo's new BZL electric single-deckers, bodied by MCV.

Awarded another seven years on the E7, Abellio (now, of course, rebranding as Transport UK) made the decision to order Wrightbus's new GB Kite Electroliner single-decker for this busy Ealing-area route which, unlike most of its fellow E-routes, has resisted double-decking. The first examples had been seen on delivery by the end of 2023, but prior to that, Southall's ADL E20D 8872 (YX16 OFZ) is coming into Ealing on 17 August.

The 358's electrification is another matter again, with this route long enough to encounter range anxiety. To offset that, another try at opportunity charging (as already found at the Bexleyheath garage base of route 132) is being mounted, by building gantries at the 358's Crystal Palace and Orpington Station termini. It is underneath these that a new fleet of swoopy, futuristic-looking Irizar IE Trams will power themselves up between trips. They will replace Mercedes-Benz Citaros like MEC 55 (BF65 HUU), seen in Bromley town centre on 21 March 2003.

Other books you might like:

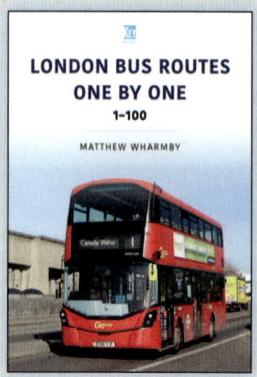
Transport Systems Series, Vol. 3

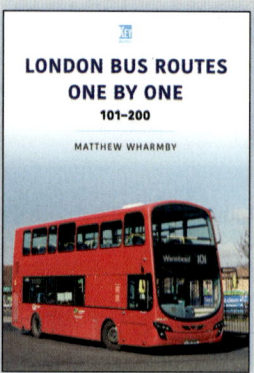
Transport Systems Series, Vol. 4

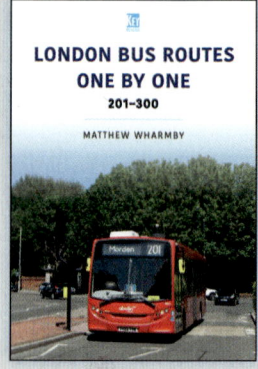
Transport Systems Series, Vol. 5

Transport Systems Series, Vol. 6

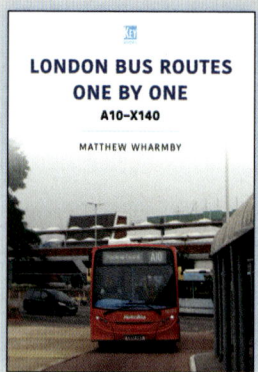
Transport Systems Series, Vol. 7

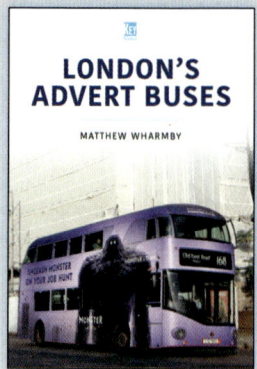
Britain's Buses Series, Vol. 15

For our full range of titles please visit:
shop.keypublishing.com/books

VIP Book Club

Sign up today and receive
TWO FREE E-BOOKS

Be the first to find out about our forthcoming book releases and receive exclusive offers.

Register now at **keypublishing.com/vip-book-club**

Our VIP Book Club is a 100% spam-free zone, and we will never share your email with anyone else. You can read our full privacy policy at: privacy.keypublishing.com